Praise for *Death at the Priory:*

"[An] account of a murder investigation that included so many elements of the best crime fiction that even Agatha Christie took a stab at solving it. In his engrossing exploration of the case, author James Ruddick burrows deeply enough to expose the cruelties beneath the façade of gentility and propriety in Victorian England."
—Mike Snyder, *Houston Chronicle*

"Ruddick may not have invented his colorful cast of characters, but he excels in displaying the raw emotions behind their actions. . . . Ruddick has given the reader a front-row seat to what in fact was a turning point in England's social history." —Brandon Whiting, *The Philadelphia Inquirer*

"Compelling . . . *Death at the Priory* reads like a first-rate murder mystery whose key points are bolstered by the author's deep knowledge of the Victorian era." —Susan Balee, *The Weekly Standard*

"A well-told tale of a murder mystery that has intrigued the English for generations . . . An absorbing melodrama. The joy in this book comes from Ruddick's clever detective work."
—Matthew Price, *The Raleigh News & Observer*

"James Ruddick's *Death at the Priory* offers a meticulously researched and utterly gripping account of Victorian murder and marriage. It bears all the hallmarks of an immensely satisfying mystery."—Elizabeth George

"*Death at the Priory* is as compelling as any fictional thriller. James Ruddick possesses a real talent for bringing the characters and the situation to fascinating life."
—Kate Atkinson, author of *Behind the Scenes at the Museum*

DEATH AT THE PRIORY

MURDER.

£250 REWARD.

WHEREAS, on the 21st April, 1876, CHARLES DELAUNEY TURNER BRAVO, of the Priory, Balham, died from the effects of Tartar Emetic, and a Coroner's Jury has returned a Verdict that the deceased was Wilfully Murdered.

The above Reward will be paid by Her Majesty's Government to any person who shall give such information and evidence as shall lead to the discovery and conviction of the Murderer or Murderers in this case, and the Secretary of State for the Home Department will advise the grant of Her Majesty's gracious PARDON to any accomplice, not being the person who actually committed the Murder, who shall give such evidence as shall lead to a like result.

Information to Superintendent Williamson, Detective Office, Great Scotland Yard, London, S.W.

E. Y. W. HENDERSON,

Commissioner of Police of the Metropolis.

Metropolitan Police Office, 4, Whitehall Place,
14th August, 1876.

Death at the Priory

LOVE, SEX AND MURDER IN
VICTORIAN ENGLAND

James Ruddick

GROVE PRESS
New York

First published in Great Britain in 2001 by Atlantic Books

Published simultaneously in Canada
Printed in the United States of America

FIRST GROVE PRESS EDITION

Library of Congress Cataloging-in-Publication Data

Ruddick, James.
    Death at the Priory : love, sex, and murder in Victorian England /
James Ruddick.
       p. cm.
    Includes bibliographical references and index.
    ISBN 0-8021-3974-4 (pbk.)
    1. Bravo, Charles Delaunay Turner, 1845–1876. 2. Bravo, Florence,
1845–1878. 3. Murder—England—London. 4. Poisoning—England—
London. I. Title.

HV6535.G73 L67 2002
364.15'23'0942166—dc21   2001022522

Grove Press
841 Broadway
New York, NY 10003

03 04 05 06 07   10 9 8 7 6 5 4 3 2 1

For Fred Earnshaw
Actor, philosopher, bon viveur, *friend.*

CONTENTS

LIST OF ILLUSTRATIONS

ACKNOWLEDGEMENTS

This book started life as a series of research papers written while I was in the Department of English and Related Literature, the University of York. Thanks are due to all those at York who encouraged me with the project, particularly Professor James Walvin, of the Department of History, who was helpful and interested throughout, and Dr Keith Alderman, Senior Lecturer in the Department of Politics, who was always available for advice and support. Thanks are also due to the staff of the J. B. Morrell Library at the University of York; to the staff of the Wellcome Institute Library; the British Library; the British Newspaper Library, Colindale; the Library of the Royal College of Medicine; Michael Lea, Librarian at the College of Law, York; Richard Shaw, Local History Librarian at Balham Library; Sheila Simmons of Malvern Library; the staff of the Public Record Office, Kew; the staff of Somerset House, and of the General Register Office, St Catherine's House, London.

In my search for the Campbell family I owe special thanks to Richard Clay, estate manager of Buscot Park; to Jim Brown, a local historian at Buscot; and to John Gray of Faringdon. I also wish to acknowledge the co-operation of the Foreign and Commonwealth Office and of the Barbados High Commission. In my search for the Ricardo family I wish to acknowledge the assistance and co-operation of Richard Orr-Ewing of Exbury House, Hampshire, and of Richard Hall, of Didier Aaron, the Rothschild family archivist, who checked records for me.

Having traced surviving descendants of those involved, I owe special thanks to the following people who gave me access to family records, private papers and diaries, or assisted in some other way. From the Campbell family, Alison Harris and her daughter, Jacqueline; Diana McManaway, great-grand-daughter of William Campbell, brother of Florence; Susan Cambridge; and Angus and Alison Gordon. I also owe thanks to John Macdonald, a friend of the family, and a historian of the Campbell lineage. From the Ricardo family, I wish to thank Lt. Col. Peter Ricardo, MBE, for taking time out of his public inquiry to assist me; Muriel Polglase, daughter of the late Frank Ricardo; Patrick Polglase, for clambering around the attics of Albion House on my behalf; and Christopher Ricardo, who assisted me during my time in Australia.

For their help in locating and making available records, files and documents in their archives in the United Kingdom, I wish to thank the following: Lady Nairne, granddaughter of Charles Bravo's friend, Edward Hope, and her son, Viscount Mersey, who arranged for records to be checked in the Library at the House of Lords; Alison Pitzbland, Kate Woodward and Richard Sharpe at Scotland Yard, who dealt with my inquiries about the Metropolitan Police and Home Office files on the case; Linda Webb of Lewisham Borough Council, for checking records relating to the Cox family; Simon Evans, Deputy Editor of the *Malvern Gazette*; and David Edwards, senior news reporter on the paper. I owe special thanks to Dr Andrew Haynes, senior lecturer in Law, Wolverhampton University; Ian Dugdale, for his assistance with the manuscript; Dr Ben Jacoby; Dr John Harcup, author and Malvern GP; Dr John Vale, Director of the West Midlands Poisons Unit; Professor Mary Hartman, Director of the Women's Studies Institute, Rutgers University, USA; and Dr Gad Heuman, Warwick University, who provided me with information about the Honourable Henry Cox. I also wish to acknowledge the help of Cora Weaver, Elizabeth Jenkins and Richard Whittington Egan.

I wish to thank the following for their endeavours and their support in researches in Jamaica: the Director and his staff at the National Library of Jamaica, Kingston; Elizabeth Williams and Michele Creed-Nelson, Acting Government Archivists at the Jamaica National Archives and Records Office, Spanish Town; Dr Patrick Bryan, former Chairman of the History Department, the University of the West Indies; and Professor Barry Higman, Senior Lecturer in the Department of History, the University of the West Indies. Many people in the parish of St Ann gave me help with information on the Cox family and their plantation estates: Peter Hall, Managing Director of the Jamaica Inn, located Mrs Cox's third home, Carlton, for me, in the district of Moneague. Juliet Shim, Marlon Maitland and Leaford Davis made inquiries on my behalf in the vicinity of Ocho Rios and St Ann's Bay, while my friend, Tony Carr, exercising limitless patience, accompanied me on a long excursion into the interior around Golden Spring and Claremont. The discovery of Mrs Cox's colonial estates, Content and Endeavor, is entirely due to Tony's relentless persistence.

Finally, on a personal note, I must thank my great friend, Nicola Burdett, for her enthusiasm for this project; Toby Mundy and Alice Hunt at Atlantic Books, who worked tirelessly to bring it to fruition, and my partner, Suzanna, who entertained Charles and Florence for more than a year with only occasional complaint.

On a warm April morning in 1876, the body of a young barrister named Charles Bravo was carried out of a house in Balham, south London. Six doctors, including Queen Victoria's physician, had attempted to save him, but he had died after suffering 'three days of the most terrible agony'. His intestines had been burnt and blistered by a highly irritant poison. The cause of death was eventually diagnosed as heart failure, produced by the suppressant effect of the poison on the central nervous system. Bravo had just turned thirty. At his bedside when he died were his wife, mother, and cousin, none of whom had been able to establish why he should have swallowed an irritant poison, or to identify what the poison was.

Within a week, the police had decided that Bravo's death was not, as they had originally thought, a simple case of suicide. Subsequently a file was opened at Scotland Yard, and two senior detectives were assigned to trace the murderer. Almost at once, the police narrowed their inquiries down to a handful of suspects. There was Charles Bravo's wife, Florence, the young and beautiful daughter of a famous industrialist. Florence's brief marriage to Bravo had been a turbulent one, and their domestic relations had become increasingly hostile. The police also discovered that Florence was one of the few people with an opportunity to administer the poison.

Then there was the couple's housekeeper, Jane Cox, who had been facing dismissal at Bravo's hands, and whose behaviour on the night of his collapse aroused considerable suspicion. One of the most interesting and surprising suspects was the celebrated Victorian physician, James Gully. Gully – confidant to the rich and famous, whose patients included Charles Dickens, Florence Nightingale, the two prime ministers, Disraeli and Gladstone, and the botanist, Charles Darwin – had had a long love affair with Florence Bravo before her marriage. It was popularly claimed that he bore a grudge against Bravo for stealing his mistress, and, as a physician, had had unlimited access to the rare poison that had been used to kill him.

In an effort to unravel the mystery, a Coroner's inquest was held, in which the greatest legal minds of the day scrutinized the various suspects. The Attorney General himself appeared for the Crown, while Florence was represented by Sir Henry James, Gladstone's former Solicitor General. The inquest proved to be one of the most sensational legal dramas of the nineteenth century. In court, not only were the various motives and theories explored, but the details of Florence's affair with Gully were exposed for the first time, including the revelation that, while holidaying together in Austria, Florence had become pregnant by the doctor, and that he had performed an abortion on her. Confessions of sexual misconduct, extracted from various witnesses in moments of high courtroom drama, produced unprecedented public interest. *The Times* branded the inquest 'the most disgusting exhibition to have been witnessed in this generation'. But the central question was to remain unanswered. After five weeks of inquiry the jury announced that there was 'insufficient evidence' to name Charles Bravo's murderer, and all the suspects were duly acquitted.

The jury's verdict, its careful ambiguity, meant that the Bravo mystery won a lasting place in the chronicles of English domestic crime. Although a steady stream of books and television pro- grammes appeared over the next hundred years, expounding numerous hypotheses of what might have happened, no convincing solution to the mystery was ever produced. Indeed, the story gradually acquired all the resonance of a classic unsolved murder, exerting a strange, magnetic power over those who came into contact with it. 'Few more baffling mysteries,' wrote Cyril Connolly, 'have entered the annals of crime.' Agatha Christie thought it was 'one of the most mysterious poisoning cases ever recorded'. For William Roughead it remained 'the prize puzzle of British criminal jurisprudence'. By the time of the hundredth anniversary of Bravo's death, when the BBC screened a major television series on the case, and yet more books were published, it was clear that the mystery would never be solved.

That changed, however, in the late 1990s. In the autumn of 1999, I began the biggest historical investigation of the case ever conducted – an investigation that was eventually to reveal the true story of what had really happened to Charles Bravo.

My interest in the case had been accidental. I had been researching a series of seminar papers on the Victorians in the Department of English and Related Literature at the University of York. The Balham Mystery (as it was popularly known) had occurred at a moment of immense social change, when the middle classes were evolving into their modern shape, and the story offered a glimpse of the way in which abstract historical events had touched the lives of real people. The cast included a gallery of characters – merchants, landowners, politicians, servants – whose day-to-day lives, suddenly exposed by the traumatic events of that night, told their own idiosyncratic stories of nineteenth-century England. But this dry inquiry turned out to be merely the prelude to a much longer struggle for the truth. In due course, revisiting the case as a broadcast journalist, I became hooked by the mechanics of the mystery, the intractable nature of the puzzle, the monomania of logistics and motives. I resolved when I began my investigation that a new approach to the conundrum was needed. Everything that had been published on the case drew solely on the records of the Coroner's inquest. Consequently, they revealed nothing new, and they got no nearer to the truth than the original inquiry had done. In order to make any breakthroughs I decided that it would be necessary to scrap all the secondary accounts of the story and to return, as far as possible, to the original sources. I therefore acquired access to the files held by the Metropolitan Police and by the Home Office. I studied the reports of the investigating officers, the findings of scientific experts, and the statements of witnesses. I had privileged access to the forensic reports of the leading physicians involved in the case –

evidence that has remained concealed in the files of the Royal College of Physicians for over a century.

The following year the hunt went worldwide. I travelled to Jamaica, where a significant part of the story had unfolded, to unearth documents buried in the vaults of the National Archives. At the same time I set about tracking down the descendants of those who had been involved. I travelled to the Pacific Rim in search of members of Florence Bravo's family, who were dotted around Australia and New Zealand. My inquiries in Sydney and Nelson generated a mass of fresh material, including unpublished letters and family papers. It was on this global trail that I discovered the new evidence which has enabled me to expose Charles Bravo's murderer.

Yet the saga of Bravo's death also lay bedded upon another deep seam: the story of the private lives of Victorian men and women, played out behind closed doors.

Florence Bravo's propulsion into the public arena took place against a background of widely circumscribed rights for women, who were excluded from universities and the professions, often the reluctant partners in arranged marriages, and who were subjected to domestic isolation once they had fulfilled their maternal duties. It emerged that Florence Bravo had used her tremendous wealth and her social position to exert a degree of control over her life that was almost unheard of in Victorian Britain, and which antagonized entrenched traditions. Florence ran her own household, managed her own financial affairs, and – as her illicit affair with the doctor proved – made choices about her lifestyle which were outside the parameters of social, moral and legal convention. The storm of popular attack that rained down on her when her secrets were finally exposed revealed a great deal about the governing imperatives of British society.

The narrative shape of the book reflects these disparate threads. The first part is a straight summary of the events that led to the fatal night. It examines the historical dimensions of the case, and enshrines a single, powerful moment of British social history. The second part outlines my own inquiries into the murder, and, through an analysis of the new evidence, gradually pieces together the true story of what actually happened in the Bravo house on that night in 1876. At times, these strands of the plot intertwine, although it is not until the last moment that the complete story finally comes into focus.

I

'The Strange Death of a Rising Young Barrister'

Here was the sharpest of all lines of social division, between those who were and those who were not respectable: a sharper line by far than that between rich and poor, employer and employee, or capitalist and proletarian. To be respectable in mid-Victorian Britain had the same cachet as being a good party man in a communist state. It signified at one and the same time intrinsic virtue and social value. The respectable man was a good man, and also a pillar of society. He might be poor, he might be rich: it really made no matter.

GEOFFREY BEST, Mid-Victorian Britain

CHAPTER ONE

The Bridge of Sighs

The physician should control, and not pander to, his patient.
DR JAMES GULLY, *The Water Cure in Chronic Disease*

Florence Campbell would never forget the first time she saw Alexander Ricardo. Even years later, after suffering prolonged abuse at his hands, she would remember that night and speak of it with a fondness that surprised people. He had been standing with a group of officers, wearing the grey-green colours of the Grenadier Guards. 'He was a very dashing and handsome boy,' said Peter Ricardo, a descendant of his family. 'He had no shortage of female admirers.'

Twelve years later, speaking to her father's secretary about that night, Florence could recall every detail: how she had effected an introduction; how they had danced together three times and then gone out onto the balcony, away from the other guests. Ricardo was the model of a military hero, straight out of a novel by Jane Austen. His hair was thick and black and cut short. His face was lean, with dark eyes and heavy, hooded brows. Florence told her sister Edith that he looked Byronic. She was dazzled by handsome men – it was a joke between the sisters – and Alexander was 'easily' the most handsome she had ever met.

As they sat on the balcony, she said, she picked her way carefully over his credentials: his father was a Liberal MP, he told her, and his mother was a great society beauty, the sister of the Duke of Fife. 'He told me that he had been in the army all his life, since a boy,' she said later, 'although his family wanted him to take up business.' Now twenty-two, Ricardo had been stationed in Canada, at the Royal Military College, for two years.

The following day Florence spoke to her father. It was done carefully, discreetly. Most young women of her generation had perfected paternal relations into an art form. And Florence had to be more careful than most. Robert Campbell was a staunch Protestant, a Calvinist, who regarded the selection of a suitable marriage partner for his daughters as of equal importance to expanding his vast commercial empire. But Campbell liked the sound of Ricardo. He knew of the family – John Ricardo, the boy's father, had founded the International Telegraph Company – and his mother was a neighbour of theirs in Belgravia. He asked Florence to bring the captain to lunch.

For Alexander Ricardo the attractions of nineteen-year-old Florence Campbell were obvious. Her auburn hair was long and rich, styled in the close ringlets that were then just becoming fashionable amongst actresses such as Ellen Terry and Sarah Fielding. She had a voluptuous figure, which she accentuated with impossibly tight dresses from Collard and Jay's. Her eyes were a cool, dispassionate grey, framed by small, fragile features. It was the kind of face, looking at it now, which must have aroused masculine protectiveness.

As a child Florence had been infuriatingly stubborn, sulking for days when she didn't get her own way. She kept that characteristic in adulthood, and people remarked on how headstrong and determined she was. But there was a vulnerability to her also, a kind of inner fragility. She adored animals, particularly horses, and often seemed to retreat into their world when she was anxious or upset. Her mother remembered how her eighteenth birthday had been ruined by the death of a family pet, which she had mourned for weeks.

One of the most striking things about Florence was her voice. She had spent her early years in Australia, following her father around the various mines owned by the Campbell family, and she could apparently pass for one of the Adelaide population. Yet all her relatives spoke with Scottish accents, and as she grew up their dialect affected her as well. To complicate matters further, she was given elocution lessons as a teenager. The result was an accent that seemed to belong to the English upper classes, but which would meander back to her formative origins when it came across certain words.

Robert Campbell liked Captain Ricardo and gave permission for him to court his daughter. When the time came for them to leave Canada, Ricardo arranged for three months' leave and spent the summer at the family's country house, Buscot Park, in Berkshire. Buscot still stands today, a vast Palladian mansion, with square Georgian windows and Regency columns. The park must have been at its most beautiful then. Campbell had designed a huge lake that powered a new distillery, and had built an arbour and water garden.

Six weeks later, at the beginning of August, the couple became engaged. The wedding was fixed for 21 September 1864. The newspapers talked excitedly of a union between two great families of Europe. The Ricardos were Dutch Jews, of enormous antiquity and grandeur, while the Campbells were Scottish landowners. 'The service is to take place at Buscot church,' said an Oxfordshire newspaper, 'and is to be conducted by Samuel Wilberforce.'

After the honeymoon, which was spent on the Rhine, the couple returned to England and took up residence at a sumptuous house in the West Country. An idyllic life seemed to stretch ahead. Robert Campbell gave his daughter a marriage settlement of £1,000 a year, and loaned the couple his houses in Brighton and London during the holiday season. But by the spring, barely seven months into the marriage, he received word from his daughter that things were already going wrong.

The kernel could be traced back to a discussion that had taken place on the honeymoon. Florence had told Alexander that she wanted him to give up his career in the military. He was married now and the next natural step was to have children – lots of children. A military career did not fit with his civilian responsibilities, she said, it made a secure family life impossible.

It was barely nine years since Britain had been beaten back in one of the worst military conflicts of the century: conditions for troops in the Crimea had been appalling; casualties had been high; the Light

Brigade had been wiped out in a disastrous charge at Balaclava. The British army continued to sustain imperial interests in southern Africa, India, Australia and the Far East. Tensions ran high between the nation states of Europe, busy carving up Africa. It was a dangerous time to wear a uniform. What if Alexander was sent abroad? What if he was lost in conflict? It was more than likely, Florence argued; it was highly probable.

For Alexander the army had been a way of life. He had never done anything else. He could see his wife's point of view – he was his father's only son and there was a duty to further the lineage. But there was little in civilian life to attract him. He had no interest in business or commerce; politics bored him; the old professions – medicine, law, academia – left him cold.

In the spring of 1868 Alexander obtained an honourable discharge from the Grenadier Guards. Florence had finally won him over. The couple moved to Gatcombe Park and started a round of leisured, aristocratic pursuits: hunting, fishing, horse-riding. They gave regular parties and Alexander amused himself with occasional regimental dinners. But they were to prove futile diversions. He tried to involve himself in the family business – the International Telegraph Company was setting up an operation in northern Europe. He also found investors for Robert Campbell's new method of industrialized farming. But these pursuits almost always petered out. Alexander, rootless and bored, felt adrift without his regiment. He grew irritable and depressed. He and Florence began to argue. Within a year the whole edifice of the marriage was under strain.

Soon after his discharge, Florence discovered that Alexander was seeing another woman. Gossip from the servants confirmed that he had been sleeping with a girl who lived in the West End. Rumours also reached her that he had been seen with women at hotels in Sussex and the West Country. Florence confronted Alexander, who initially denied the stories. Later he confessed and promised to end the affairs. But his fidelity was always short-lived. He was good-looking and adventurous, much desired by women, whom he also found irresistible.

At the same time, Alexander's drinking began to get out of control. He had always been a heavy drinker – his friends were notorious dilettantes, and drinking was a way of life in the army, a test of masculinity. But now it seemed that Alexander couldn't function without it. 'It became apparent that he was dependent upon his brandy,' Florence recalled.

On several occasions Florence 'remonstrated' with her husband, imploring him to pull himself together and get his life in order. 'I pleaded with him to stop drinking,' she said. But nothing worked. On one occasion he was knocked down by a carriage on a country road and spent six weeks in bed. He experienced a terrifying attack of delirium tremens during his recuperation. But it didn't cure him. It was as if he had pressed a self-destruct button; as if he was on a collision course with the dark sides of his own personality.

'Our relationship was under great strain,' Florence said. 'I was very happy with him when we first met. He was very kind. But he gradually became more and more abusive – always attacking me and saying terrible things.' The terrible things were numerous – that he should never have married her; that she didn't understand him; that she had trapped him; that she controlled him; that she had ruined his life. 'Captain Ricardo said many mad things when he was drunk,' recalled Florence's mother. Florence came to the conclusion that her husband was a deeply troubled man, hiding behind a veneer of respectability, who was tortured by self-loathing. Only the army's rigid discipline, the security of its structure and routines, had kept Alexander afloat.

Looking back, Florence's reaction to her marital problems had something ritualized about it: at first she denied the problems existed and made excuses for her husband. When she could no longer lie, not even to herself, she ran away, spending weeks alone at her father's villa in Brighton, or touring the coast with friends. Finally – when her nerves were in shreds – she succumbed to a still rage. 'I did not know from one day to the next what state he would be in,' she said. 'I never knew whether he would abuse me when he came home at night. I could not even speak to him without being abused.

I grew extremely depressed and ill.' She made up her mind to leave him.

The moment came just before Christmas, 1870. She was 'reproaching' her husband for insulting her sister during a lunch party, and his mood gradually darkened. Eventually he snapped, striking his wife in the face, three times. She screamed and struck at him with a hand mirror. Chairs were overturned. The valet rushed into the room and restrained his employer. It was a climactic scene: the effective end of a marriage. Florence packed a suitcase and summoned a carriage to take her at once to Buscot. It was nine o'clock at night and the journey took five hours, along treacherous and obscure roads.

Florence's parents were shocked by the sight of the thin and trembling girl who arrived on their doorstep. 'It was clear that my daughter had had a nervous collapse,' said Mrs Campbell. They took her into the drawing room, listened as she told them how Alexander had beaten her, and then called a doctor. Two hours later she went up to her old bedroom and slept.

Florence's return presented Robert Campbell with a fashionable dilemma. Campbell cared deeply for his daughter. 'He called her "little Florrie",' said Diana McManaway, Campbell's great-great-granddaughter, whom I interviewed in New Zealand. 'She was his favourite and he had spoilt her as a child.' But Campbell could not tolerate the idea of a man and wife being formally separated. Florence's decision to leave her husband was 'morally offensive', he believed, and could not be sanctioned. In the morning he told her that she had a duty to stand by her husband, regardless of his behaviour, and that he would arrange for her to be sent back to London. He promised to speak to Alexander as a compromise. At this point Florence became hysterical. Her father's reaction mined that deep seam of stubbornness that had been inside her since childhood. 'She said she would not return to Alexander under any circumstances,' recalled her mother. 'She would leave the house and never come back if we insisted.' Eventually Mrs Campbell intervened. She suggested that Florence go away for a while – alone – so that she could recuperate and reassess her feelings. That might also shock Alexander into reform. Florence could be admitted into the Hydro, a high-class sanatorium, run by the famous physician, James Gully. When she felt better she could make a proper decision about her future.

It was a typical Victorian compromise – postponing the issue, finding a formula on which everyone could agree. Florence saw it as her only realistic option, and so, three days later, she arrived at Dr Gully's clinic in Malvern, the Worcestershire spa town on the Welsh borders.

Life at the Hydro reminded Florence of growing up. She had been raised at Buscot Park, a ten-bedroom mansion surrounded by 3,000 acres of parkland. She had swum in the lake, walked down to the church every Sunday, played in the woods with her sisters. It had been a remarkably insular and relaxed childhood. The Hydro had that feeling of shelter, too. Its atmosphere was designed to protect its patients from all the stresses of their highly industrialized society. The clinic was large and roomy, Tudor in origin, with fine Regency furnishings. Patients had private rooms, looking across to the church and the promenade gardens, and could wander over its endless manicured lawns. Newspapers were banned. So were visitors. Inside, time stopped and the problems of the world seemed comfortably remote.

On her arrival Florence exchanged her corsets and satin gowns for a plain cotton dress, loose-fitting and airy. She began a daily routine that was regimented: baths at seven-thirty, a walk on the hills before breakfast, a light meal, tennis in the afternoon, a swim before dinner, and then bed at nine. Her diet was rigid, too: the social poisons were banned – sugar, tea, coffee and alcohol – replaced by spring water, wholemeal bread, fish and vegetables. The staff encouraged her to sit in the drawing room and meet the other patients, to talk over her problems freely in a supportive atmosphere. There she met women like herself: lonely, idle, sexually repressed women whose self-esteem had been shattered at the hands of their husbands.

At the end of the week Florence had her first consultation with the

Hydro's director. Dr Gully had first met her when she was a child of twelve. 'I had known Robert and Anne Campbell for thirty years,' he said. 'I had treated the whole family. I first saw her as a child when she came to me with a throat infection. During that time she would visit my surgery and take tea with me.'

Gully must have cut an impressive figure, seated at a vast walnut desk in the dense stillness of his surgery. He was a small man, now in his mid-sixties, bald and pale. His face had never been handsome, not even in his youth, and now it was plump and lined. But in his features he had a gentleness, a soothing strength, that was striking to see. The Prime Minister, Lord Aberdeen, said he was 'the most gifted physician of the age', while Charles Darwin called him 'my beloved friend'. His manner exuded a quiet charisma. When he spoke, his voice was cultured and warm. People remarked on his ability to charm small children out of their screaming fits, or to soothe the palpitations of people who brought him their hysteria.

Women in particular seemed to find Dr Gully attractive. When they went to see their own physicians – with the vague symptoms of depression and anxiety so prevalent in Victorian England – they usually received a uniform dispensation: they should concentrate on being better wives, on fulfilling their marital duties. They should pull themselves together and count their blessings. If the physician was severe enough in his thunder the women would go home shaken and subdued. They would resume their quiet lives without a word. But eventually the reprimand would wear off, the old problems would resurface, and the women would again crowd into the surgery.

Gully's views were very different. He had learned long ago to abandon stern remedies in favour of a more progressive approach. He did not see women as other men saw them – as little more than domestic slaves, needing only to have children in order to be fulfilled human beings. Instead, he believed that all kinds of female neurosis – hysteria, depression, anxiety, hypochondria – were actually unconscious responses to the pressures that women were under: pressure to be chaste and pure, to be ambitionless and domestically efficient; the pressure to think of their husbands and children but never of themselves. 'All these pressures are worsened by their boredom,' he wrote, 'and their lack of sexual satisfaction.'

Gully spent two hours with Florence. He knew at once that she was a model patient. She was obsessed by her health and the minor ailments that afflicted her. She couldn't concentrate. She wept uncontrollably. Hundreds of such women had come and gone over the years. Gradually she went over the story of her disastrous marriage – Alexander's womanizing and alcoholism; his failed attempts at reform; her own depression; her father's harsh response to her situation.

At the end of the meeting Gully startled his patient. He announced that there was only one course of action that would be effective in helping her. She must find the strength to defy her father and separate completely from her husband. Nothing else would work. 'I had not seen Captain Ricardo as a patient,' he said. 'But it seemed to me that he was beyond reform, and I advised Mrs Ricardo to separate from him. I promised to assist her in that separation in whatever way I could.' Gully said that if Florence was willing to do this he would make himself her legal guardian and arrange for the separation papers to be drawn up. He would instruct his lawyers to secure an annual alimony payment from her husband and allow her to remain at the Hydro free of charge.

Florence could barely believe her luck. She had decided long ago that her marriage to Alexander was over. But she could see no way out of the situation. Now she was being offered the protection of a powerful man, a man whose status and resources equalled those of her own father. 'I was grateful to him for taking the situation in hand,' she said. 'I felt that a great burden had been lifted from me.'

Florence wrote to her husband immediately, informing him that she was not coming home. She also wrote to her family, asking them to respect her decision. As is often the case in an abusive marriage, Alexander reformed the moment he realized that his wife was sincere in her intent. But by then it was too late, as it always is. His telegrams went unanswered. His letters were left to gather dust on the dressing table. When he arrived at the Hydro he was informed that Florence would not see him and ejected by the two men who ran the pump rooms. A month later he went abroad.

With Ricardo's shadow lifting, and her own health improving, the way was clear for Florence to start a new life. Gully had succeeded in negotiating a settlement for her with the Ricardo family, giving her a measure of financial security. He told her that he would arrange for her to be discharged from the clinic as soon as her separation had been ratified. But Florence said that she had nowhere to go. She could not return to Buscot. Her father had made it clear that she was not welcome there. She had no friends outside her husband's social circle. Her brother William lived in Surrey, but he was married and had his own life. 'I was completely alone and isolated,' she recalled.

Gully arranged for Florence to rent a house in Malvern, where she could keep in touch with the women she had met at the Hydro, and visit him from time to time to discuss her progress.

What Florence had not told Gully, however, was that she did not wish to start a new life because she could not face leaving him. She was already under his spell, within his aura. In fact Florence had decided that she was in love with Dr Gully.

It had not been a sudden, blinding realization. It had been slow and steady, from a seed of mere gratitude – and a gentle awakening to his charms. 'He is the cleverest man I have ever met,' she wrote. During her treatment she had taken to lunching with him. Once or twice they had had dinner together. Then, one afternoon in the spring, he had suggested that they walk on the Malvern Hills, up to Willow Cresent, his favourite point, so that they could admire the views. For the first time he had actually spoken about himself. They had settled on the grass and he had chatted to her about his past, his career in medicine, his family. Florence remembered it later as the moment when a professional relationship became a mutual friendship – and when she began to fall in love, really in love, for the first time in her life. 'He told me how he had been born into money but his family had lost it all when he was a boy,' she recalled. 'He said it was the best thing that ever happened to him because it forced him to get out and earn a living.' Gully explained how he had trained in Paris, how he had become disillusioned with the rigid orthodoxy of Western medicine. He told her that he had studied country folklore, herbalism and spiritual healing. His approach was holistic and increasingly maverick. But he was not a quack. His life had been changed overnight, he admitted, when he had read a paper advocating something called hydrotherapy – the use of water to cure physical disease. Hydrotherapy provided a focus for his discontent with modern practices, and an opportunity to innovate a treatment that he believed was rooted in scientific principles. He had moved to Malvern the following year, a town already famous for its mountain spas. By 1850 he had published many books and was receiving patients from America and Europe.

But it was not just Gully's professional status that had attracted Florence. She found that he had a magnetic personality, too. One evening in March she had heard him give a lecture to Malvern's civic leaders. She sat in the audience in the small town hall, surrounded by businessmen and newspaper reporters, and listened to him urging people to support public services. His gift of oration thrilled her. She wrote to her sister the next day, describing the event. A week later Gully gave her a copy of a play he had written – *A Night in the Bastille* – which had run successfully at Drury Lane. Florence told her sister that Gully's friends included two prime ministers, an array of scientists, and many figures from the worlds of art, literature and music. Tennyson, she said, went to him year in, year out, without fail. Queen Victoria studied his theories and took the treatments he prescribed. So did Florence Nightingale, whom he had once saved from a nervous breakdown. At the time he was treating Florence he was also treating Charles Darwin, who had come to him with a severe chest infection. ('Gully has made me stop taking snuff,' Darwin complained, 'my chief solace in life.')

Florence now began to make inquiries about Gully's private life. She knew she was crossing a dangerous rubicon. Her sister – sensing her romantic designs – had advised her to leave Malvern immediately. No good could come of her growing infatuation. But

Florence's desire was now overpowering. She learned from another physician at the Hydro that Gully was married. But later she discovered that his wife was in her eighties, that they had been separated for thirty years, and that her family had confined her to a mental institution. Gully had grown-up children living in London, and his household was run by his two sisters. Yet in spite of his wealth and his social eminence, there were no women in his life. In fact he seemed to be settling down to a comfortable old age. The news excited her enormously – even more so because she could not share it with anyone.

In August, Gully told Florence that he was undertaking a research visit to Kissingen, a small town in rural Bavaria. He asked her to go with him and Florence seized the opportunity. They travelled under their own names, taking their servants with them. They booked into separate rooms, staying at Madame Manteuffel's hotel in Bodenlaube. They toured the mountain ranges where modern water therapy had begun, walking each evening through the shaded avenues of the Kur Garten, taking hundreds of mineral samples from the springs and the peat hills. Then, two days into the holiday, Florence decided that her moment had come. She gave her servant, Humphries, the day off. After lunch she announced that she was retiring to her room for an afternoon nap, and asked Gully to sit with her. According to an account that she gave later, she lay on the bed, half-dressed, and chatted to the doctor as he sat near her in the chair. At one point she reached out to take his hand and then drew him towards her. He kissed her, got up, and closed the curtains. Then he undressed. They made love twice before falling asleep. Later, a domestic servant was asked:

Q: At this time, was Mrs Ricardo very intimate with Dr Gully?
(Pause)
A: Well, he often called round to the house.
Q: Did he treat Mrs Ricardo with a good deal of familiarity?
A: He treated her as a gentleman treats a lady.
Q: Did you look upon Dr Gully as Mrs Ricardo's friend? Or did you look upon him as her lover?

(Silence)

Q: Did you look upon Dr Gully merely as a friend or did you regard him as her lover?
(Silence)

Q: I must put it to you again: did you regard Gully as Mrs Ricardo's lover?

A: Dr Gully was very much interested in her.

Q: *Did you know that Dr Gully was her lover?* You lived there. You must have had a shrewd idea. Did you think that Dr Gully was Mrs Ricardo's lover?

A: Yes, I suppose I did.
(Sensation)

Both of them knew the enormous risks that they were taking by allowing their relationship to become sexual. Sex outside marriage offended common decency and transgressed a strict moral code. Sex between two people who were already married made it worse. And sex between two people, already married, who were separated by more than a generation, was a shocking perversion. Their society would be merciless in its judgement if they were ever exposed. Yet to both of them it seemed worth the risk. 'I was very much in love with her,' said Dr Gully. 'I loved him very deeply,' said Florence.

And there was no point pretending that what had just happened in that remote hotel in Germany would stop there. Florence's sex life with Alexander, crippled by alcoholism, had never been very fulfilling. Now she was in the hands of a man whose capacity for the physical expression of his feelings was much more developed. She was awakening.

On their return to England the couple began sleeping together regularly – while always maintaining the appearance of a rather distant platonic relationship. Gully took dinner with Florence but would always leave the house by 10 p.m. He would sometimes return after midnight, when the servants had gone to bed. Occasionally they would arrange liaisons in the very early morning, or go out on the Malvern Hills and rendezvous at a secret place. They were shaken only once, when a servant inadvertently stumbled upon them having sex in Florence's bedroom. They dressed quickly and Florence caught up with the girl on the stairs, swearing her to secrecy. Later she bribed the girl into silence. 'I will do everything I can to secure you a good position,' she wrote, when the maid decided to leave. 'I hope you will never tell anyone of what happened at Malvern. It is all buried in the past. If anyone ever questions you, refuse to answer their questions.' She ended in block capitals: 'BURN THIS.'

Once the relationship had become sexual the couple regarded themselves as privately engaged. Two weeks after they came back from Kissingen, Gully asked Florence to marry him. He told her that they would wait for his wife to die rather than invite a scandal. Then they would marry in England and would go to live abroad. In the meantime, they had to work hard at keeping their affair secret.

On 20 April 1871, when her affair with Gully was only a few months old, Florence received a telegram from London. Alexander, it announced, was dead. He had collapsed in a hotel room in Cologne and the post-mortem confirmed haematemesis, brought on by alcoholism. 'The doctors had warned him that the coats of his stomach were going,' recalled Mrs Campbell. Florence could feel no real sense of loss. 'He had died for me years ago,' she said. But the news was to affect her, nonetheless, in a profound way. Four days later she was told by Ricardo's solicitor that he had neglected to change his will after their separation, which meant that Florence was still his chief beneficiary. When she asked how much he had left her the answer produced a second of disbelief. 'Around forty thousand pounds,' replied the solicitor, Mr Berger. 'For a moment I couldn't believe it,' she would tell her niece.

The change in Florence's fortunes was remarkable; less than a year earlier she had worried that she had nowhere to go as a separated woman; now she was rich, fabulously rich, even by the standards of her own wealthy family. In an age when the average couple lived on £30 a year, Florence had a personal fortune running into tens of thousands. She could invest the money in stocks and shares, even in low-return bank accounts, and live quite comfortably on the interest.

She immediately decided to leave Malvern and move to London – provided Gully would go with her. She loved the time that she had spent in the capital; her family had a mansion in Belgravia where she had lived for six weeks each year. She loved the theatres, the lights of the West End, the opera and ballet. Malvern was pretty enough, but London was the home of the great thinkers, the merchants and explorers, the political leaders, and the men of letters. And with her vast fortune and her great beauty she could be at the very epicentre of city life.

Eventually she decided on a large mansion in Balham, south London, called the Priory. It was half an hour away from the West End, but it was rural enough to give her a landscape view, great gardens, pretty orchards and open fields. She could indulge her passion for gardening, and she had enough land to keep horses. She would build a stable and some paddocks, she decided, and buy two horses to ride across Streatham Common.

After some hesitation James Gully agreed to accompany her. He had got used to the quiet streets of Worcestershire, and the beautiful walks around Hanley Castle and Swan Pool. But Balham was pretty, too. You could walk across Streatham fields as far as Mitcham Common and see no more than a handful of farm labourers all afternoon. And he understood that Florence was keen to enjoy the excitements of a big city. He arranged to buy a property called Orwell Lodge, on Bedford Hill Road, less than five minutes' walk from the Priory.

The Priory still stands today, and is easily the finest house in the neighbourhood. It was built at the end of the eighteenth century, in imitation gothic, with castle turrets and casement windows. Inside, a large hallway opens onto a beautiful baroque staircase, which curves elegantly up to the first floor. There was a morning room, a dining room and a library. The house was lit with gas lamps. And wherever the eye turned there was wealth: marble busts, chandeliers, English rosewood. Upstairs there was a master bedroom panelled in oak, a dressing room and a spare bedroom. There were also rooms on the second floor for the servants.

The furnishing of the new house gave a clue to Florence's compulsive desire for display and entertainment. She bought a vast ten-foot sideboard; a dining table made from Spanish mahogany, with twelve dinner chairs, each upholstered in crimson leather; three satin suites; gold candelabra; a walnut piano made by Broadwood; and a glittering collection of Venetian glass.

Over the coming weeks Florence staffed the house with a regiment of servants. She hired three young maids, a cook, a butler, two groundsmen, a coachman, a groom, a footman, and three gardeners. She also decided to employ a lady's-companion, to oversee the day-to-day running of the house. The companion's name was Mrs Cox.

Jane Cannon Cox was to make an ideal murder suspect. Georges Simenon could not have dreamt up a more perfect creation. She was described as 'a small, bird-like woman', perpetually dressed in black, always surfacing at critical moments in the story. She was forty-seven when she met Florence, although she looked older. She invariably dressed in sober, functional clothes, and wore her long ebony hair scraped back from her forehead into a tight bun. Her face had probably once been soft, and rather generous, but now it was pinched and grey, its angular appearance accentuated by a pair of square glasses. When she spoke her voice was so quiet that people frequently did not hear it. She moved about quietly, almost timidly. People spoke of her 'gliding around'. But none of this was natural, or even accidental. It was all carefully designed to make you overlook her. Perhaps you even forgot that she was there. For reasons that were obvious to the domestic servant, she cultivated invisibility.

Beneath the inscrutable exterior, however, Jane Cox was a personification of the English middle classes. Life had been especially unkind to her. Yet she rarely spoke of the miseries she had suffered, and she responded to her problems with a combination of grit and unbelievable industry.

During that first interview Mrs Cox sat in the morning room at the

Priory and went through her list of credentials. She produced refer-
ences from a curate and a solicitor. As she spoke, Florence felt herself
warming to the natural calmness, the quiet authority of the woman
in front of her. 'I was very impressed by her,' she said, later, 'particularly her kindness and her excellent manners.'

Mrs Cox told Florence that she was a widow, currently employed
as a nanny to the small children of a London solicitor. Her husband
had died in Jamaica, where they had settled soon after their marriage,
and she had decided to return to England with their three children.
She had sent the boys to a charity school and then got a job as a
governess. Later she had borrowed money from her late husband's
employer, Joseph Bravo, and bought a house in London – not to live
in, but to rent out as bedsits.

The story that Jane Cox told that spring afternoon perfectly illustrated the extent to which a single Victorian woman was generally
dependent on her own resources. When her husband died, aged
thirty, their youngest child was three, their middle child five, and
their eldest seven. It was a critical moment to have been widowed.
After his death Jane received no help from her family. She lived
frugally. Illness could not be afforded. Pennies were scratched
together in anticipation of the day she was unable to work. For those
who found themselves in this position, Victorian England was a
dangerous, truly Dickensian world: there was no social security, no
unemployment benefit, no national insurance. As a result it would be
fair to say that servants like Mrs Cox, finding a loyal and generous
employer like Florence Ricardo, would do almost anything to protect
their position. The absence of a state safety net underscored the
sense of fear and desperation that bubbled beneath the surface of
national life.

A year after Florence had agreed to employ Mrs Cox, she wrote a
letter to her which indicates the demanding role the companion had
assumed in the house:

My dearest Mrs Cox,
    Thank you very much for the kind letter that you sent.
    Will you tell Rance [the gardener] that I have no intention of

building a greenhouse and will have nothing ordered without my permission. I told MacGrath that he was not to sleep in the house and *my order is to be obeyed*. Will you write to Mrs Goswell and demand my book back. If she does not return it, tell her that I will write to her mistress. Will you find out if she is visiting, as I gave strict instructions that she was not to come at all, and you can tell Barton that it is as much as his place is worth if she does come to my house.

I am sorry to hear you are suffering from your head, but hope by this time you are feeling better.

Will you compare Peggs prices for coal with Piggots, as I should like the cellar filled before I return. I am anxious to hear of the safe arrival of the cheque I sent you; please acknowledge it at once, and if it fails to reach you, write at once to London and County Bank, Great Malvern, to stop its payment. As I have endorsed it anyone could cash it, but I hope you will get it safe.

Please tell Rance that he must manage as well as he can with the cuttings for next year – he has more shelves than he had last winter. Please see Mould for me, and tell him to take no orders from anyone but me.

I am so glad all the dogs and horses are well.

Neighbours in Balham would later recall the sight of Florence and Mrs Cox travelling together in their open-top carriage, and comment on the attraction of opposites: Florence, the beautiful young widow, with her jewellery and flowing hair; Mrs Cox, the small, shy woman, draped in black, with the hardness and the sheen of a strange insect.

Their friendship grew at a startling pace. 'We were on terms more intimate than is usual for a lady and her companion,' Mrs Cox said. 'Mrs Cox seemed to become almost one of the family,' said Florence's mother, 'and my daughter grew very attached to her.' Even the servants noticed the bond. 'Mrs Ricardo and Mrs Cox were extremely fond of each other,' said Frederick Rowe, the butler. 'They spent a great deal of time together – more time, I would say, than was usual for a mistress and her companion.'

This intimacy was partly due to the nature of the job. The lady's-companion, like the governess, enjoyed a certain status, derived from the ambiguity of her role. She was not quite a member of the family that employed her. But she certainly wasn't an ordinary domestic servant, either. She was expected to embody the high moral principles that set her apart from the vice-ridden working class, and she was rewarded with the kind of compassion and respect never afforded to an ordinary employee. But there was also a psychological dimension to this attachment. Florence was isolated from her parents and needed someone to take a maternal interest in her. 'I was very intimate with Mrs Cox,' she said. 'I called her Janie and she called me Florrie. At one time she was my only friend.'

In May 1872 the thing that Florence had most dreaded – the thing that had kept her awake at night – finally happened: her secret love affair suddenly became public. Florence had accepted an invitation to stay at the home of her solicitor, Henry Brooks, in Surrey. Brooks had been kind to her during her separation from Alexander, and had helped her with the lease of the Priory. The weekend passed pleasantly enough until the Sunday afternoon, when Mr and Mrs Brooks – who had earlier set out for a walk – returned home unexpectedly to retrieve an umbrella. In the hallway of the house they heard the unmistakable sounds of sexual activity coming from the drawing room. When they entered the room they found Florence lying on the sofa, Dr Gully beside her, both of them frantically climaxing. Dr Gully, they understood, had been visiting his friend 'to discuss a forthcoming holiday in the West Country'. After the lovers had duly collected themselves and apologized, there followed a violent scene, right there amid the religious prints and the dried flowers of Tooting suburbia.

For Henry Brooks and his wife, Florence's behaviour was beyond the pale; an unspeakable outrage. They did not, they said, expect their guest to abuse their hospitality in this way. The language grew so heated that writs were threatened and counter-threatened. Indeed, one of Mrs Brooks' remarks prompted Dr Gully to instruct his own solicitor to mount an action for slander – an instruction he subsequently withdrew.

The incident, amusing in the modern age, was a devastating

development for Florence. The servants had heard everything, and the gossip marched across south London with the speed of an epidemic. 'Mrs Ricardo's relationship with Dr Gully was soon much talked of,' said the butler. 'Everyone knew about it.' 'It became very well known in the neighbourhood,' recalled Mrs Cox, 'and people were quick to condemn.'

Florence now found herself the victim of the most vigorous Victorian disapproval. People looked at her and looked at Dr Gully and wondered how on earth she could have let herself become embroiled. Mrs Cox reported that two members of the staff were threatening to leave; some of the suppliers would not serve her when she went out for groceries. Within a week the news had reached Buscot, where it sent Robert Campbell into a state of apoplexy. 'We were aware of our daughter's infatuation with Dr Gully,' said Mrs Campbell, 'and it met with our entire disapproval.'

'He was incensed and outraged,' said Alison Harris, a descendant of his son, William. 'But behind the anger I think he was broken by the scandal. Some part of him died when he found out that his daughter had been seduced in that way.'

The civic response did not leave Florence unmoved. She complained that when she issued invitations to the Priory for dinner or for afternoon tea they were returned without explanation. Her telegrams to Buscot went unanswered. She wrote to her sister Edith in London but received no reply. In February she visited a woman friend whose husband was a business acquaintance of her father, and was turned away at the door. Wherever she went she was conscious of the hostile glare of public displeasure.

If Florence had been another kind of woman, perhaps, none of this would have mattered a great deal. But Florence had been raised as a social animal. She was educated and articulate. She enjoyed the attention of her peers, particularly male ones, and her sense of isolation was impossible to bear.

The strain on her was acknowledged by James Gully during the inquest:

Q: Did you know that Mrs Ricardo had discarded her family for you?

A: I knew she had discarded her family for me.

Q: You know that she had given up everything for you – her friends, her family – even her good name?

A: I know she had been given the choice of giving me up and had refused.

Q: You know she had given up her good name and her honour?

A: Well, she had given up her home.

Q: And her good name, her honour?
     (Pause)

A: Yes.

In order to understand the extent of Florence's 'crime', and the response to it in her society, it is necessary for us to remember how powerfully women in the Victorian age were idealized – and how far short of the ideal Florence had fallen. This was the age of the sexless Victorian woman. The English physician William Acton had identified 'the correct female' as one 'without any sexual urges'. He even claimed that women who were excited by the prospect of sexual intercourse were risking 'growths of the womb or mental depression.' In the popular mind women were delicate, ornamental and morally pure. It was widely believed that they had exceptional powers, divinely conferred, which made them immune to temptation. Men found it difficult to deal with the inescapable fact that, when they married, women actually had intercourse. They consoled themselves with the notion that they performed this act merely to attain motherhood, certainly not to satisfy low desires of lust, and that they endured it in a yawning coma of indifference.

Under these circumstances, therefore, Florence Ricardo's 'attachment' to James Gully could hardly have aroused more antipathy. She had dared not merely to engage in sexual intercourse with a married man, but, apparently, to enjoy it. 'She was a miserable woman,' complained the *Evening Standard*, 'who indulged in a disgraceful connection.' 'She was an adulteress and an inebriate,' added *The Times*, 'selfish and self-willed, a bad daughter and worse wife.'

In the spring of 1873, while the lovers tried to battle against public censure, they were suddenly confronted by another serious problem. There had been a careless night in a hotel during the Christmas holiday. Florence had drunk too much. Precautions had lapsed. And now she was sure she was pregnant. Gully came to the Priory one afternoon and confirmed it with a professional examination. Afterwards, they sat together in silence. Irritation and impatience had been picking away at them for weeks. Now the bond between them was finally ruptured, as their minds ran over the ruinous consequences that lay ahead. Gully's reputation would be destroyed. It was as simple as that. Every paper he had written, every achievement recorded in his name, would be scarred indelibly by a moment of scandal. Florence, at best, would be forced to emigrate. Almost immediately, without expression, they both knew that there was no alternative to the one that lay unspoken.

The procedure was presumably carried out at the Priory, since Mrs Cox was afterwards inveigled into acting as a nurse, carrying hot water up and down the stairs, fetching towels and ointments. But the operation seems to have gone badly wrong. Florence deteriorated within hours. She later spoke of being 'seriously ill' and claimed that her illness was life-threatening. She would not have been exaggerating. She said that she was saved only by the devotion of her companion, who nursed her tirelessly for six days and nights, sleeping in the bed with her, getting up in the night to bathe her and administer medicine. Somehow the remarkable Mrs Cox also managed to conceal the truth from the servants. She told them, without a blush of shame, that Florence was suffering from 'an unusual natural illness'. The illness arose 'from a kind of tumour, which Dr Gully had removed.'

Although the surgery saved their reputations, at least for the time being, it also destroyed their relationship. Florence refused to see Gully for two weeks after she had recovered. When she finally met him again she seized the opportunity to punish her old lover and to distance herself from him. She told him that the physical side of their affair must end, and that they should put things back onto a more formal footing. She could not engage in any kind of sexual activity. Indeed, it would be helpful to both their reputations if they saw less of each other. She consoled him with the prospect that intimacy might return in the future, and with the promise that she still loved him.

But this was kind dissimulation. Florence had had enough of her affair with James Gully and was already looking for a way out.

Soon afterwards she met Charles Bravo.

CHAPTER TWO

Games of Consequence

I have written to the doctor to tell him that I must never see his face again. It is the right thing to do.

FLORENCE RICARDO, October 1875

It is curious, looking back at the extent of the disruption wreaked upon poor Florence by life's game of consequences. There she was, at eighteen, about to embark on a perfect road – marriage, children, respectability. It was a life that would never have attracted the interest of historians or writers. Nor was it meant to do so. It was a life that would have vanished, like those of her brothers and sisters, into the obscurity of the past. But the turning of one wild card had changed everything. That wild card was Alexander, social asset and alcoholic. Alexander's behaviour had forced Florence to take refuge with her father. His rejection had pushed her into the arms of an elderly lover. Their liaison had led to social ostracism, which would, in turn, prompt Florence to pursue another man. From the moment of her first marriage, Florence's life had been reduced to a game of countermoves, in which the central player, having lost control of the deck, could do little more than react. It was almost as though *Pride and Prejudice* had been rewritten by Mary Shelley.

Charles Bravo's origins were obscure. He had been born in England in 1845, the only son of Augustus and Mary Turner. Augustus had died when Charles was a small boy and Mary had married a wealthy merchant, Joseph Bravo, who was about fifteen years her senior. Bravo had made his money with the colonial staples – fruit, tea and tobacco – and had established his reputation in

London circles in the 1850s. Charles had subsequently been educated at King's College, London, and at Oxford, and had been called to the Bar in 1868. He had adopted his stepfather's name at the age of twenty-three.

Bravo was a model of the late Victorian gentleman. He was an expert on social precedence. He studied current affairs, was energetic and reactionary, and had expressed a desire to enter Parliament. He was a member of Boodles and Whites and had been a founder of the Junior Turf Club. He was also a member of the Carlton, where his antediluvian political beliefs were institutionalized amid baroque architecture and plush Regency furnishings. After being called to the Bar, he had joined a small practice at the Temple with his friend, Edward Hope. His salary was £200 a year, a poor figure for someone with Bravo's credentials.

The meeting between Charles and Florence had been engineered by Mrs Cox. She could see how unhappy Florence was, particularly after the abortion, and how lonely she had become. What she needed was some friends, a social network, a degree of respectability. And she would only achieve these things by finding a husband.

Mrs Cox had met Charles on two or three occasions – her late husband had worked with his family in Jamaica – and she thought he would make an ideal husband for her mistress. The two women had been shopping in London just before Christmas, and had called at the Bravo house, a mansion on Palace Green, Kensington. While the little group – Florence, Mrs Cox, Joseph and Mary Bravo – had been taking tea in the vast drawing room, Charles had swept in, looking for some tobacco. Some days later Mrs Cox called again, alone this time, ostensibly as a social visit, but in reality to sell Florence to Charles's parents. She knew that Charles was single. He and Florence were social equals. They were even the same age.

A short time later Florence and Mrs Cox went to Brighton, to watch Mrs Cox's eldest son at his school sports day. Charles Bravo, she had been told, was also in Brighton, for the Quarter Sessions. A second accidental meeting, again engineered by Mrs Cox, took place when the women were strolling along the sea-front. Charles raised his hat and stopped to talk. He arranged to meet the ladies for dinner at their hotel. 'And wherever we went after that,' Florence said later, 'he was there.'

Florence was shrewd enough to know exactly what Mrs Cox was doing. But she did not resist. She was happy to let events take their course. And the more she saw of Charles Bravo the more she liked him.

Bravo was unlike either of the two men who had previously shared her life. He was cynical, witty, urbane, and devious. A photograph of him, taken on the eve of his wedding, shows a lean and rather cruel face. The camera has flashed before the subject is ready, and the lids of the eyes are caught in a blink. It gives the features a predatory look. But other photographs show a different character. Florence said that one of them made him look like a small boy.

Bravo was slim, of medium height, with brown hair and long whiskers. He dressed conservatively, fiercely resisting the latest changes in fashion. But the most remarkable thing about Bravo – and the thing that attracted Florence the most – was his amazing zest for life. 'He lived to the full,' said his stepfather. He travelled widely, read voraciously and had many diverse interests. He loved literature, particularly Shakespeare, and had a faultless knowledge of English poetry. He played chess with a passion, relishing the twists and turns of the game. He could talk confidently about politics, business, nature and history.

Yet, like many people raised in insular and protected households, Bravo lacked a sense of hinterland, a common humanity. He had enjoyed a privileged upbringing, always divided people into 'them' and 'us', and had no real sense of connection with his fellow men. He would be loyal to those within his circle. No close friend would ever be turned away, no matter what the circumstances. But he had no sense of compassion or duty to those he did not know; no pity when confronted with an abstract. 'He was ruthless in all he did,' said Florence's solicitor, later. 'He was a man of very little sentiment,' said his friend, Edward Hope. Florence, who had been raised by her Reformist father with a social conscience, a sense of paternalism, found this aspect of his character troubling. But her attraction to him was strong, nonetheless. She accompanied him to the theatre and to country houses. They spent their evenings and weekends together and toured the south coast on holiday. Bravo soon began to stay overnight at the Priory.

The correspondence that the couple wrote at this time shows a blossoming relationship: 'I approve thoroughly of what you say and do,' Bravo wrote. 'And I may tell you that I am in danger of losing my chief jewel – my modesty – when I consider that you, whose opinion I most value, has given me such high praise.' Later he wrote to his mother: 'I went to the library and brought Florence six volumes of books. She has read three of them, and the other three contain the uninspired preachings of an idiot. She has finished a pair of slippers for me, and is slanging at me for not being able to tell a good book – as you tell good music – by the look . . .' Florence also wrote to Bravo's mother, depicting a growing affection for her son. 'Charlie is looking forward to a game of lawn tennis. I never saw him look so well. The country is life to him, and he walks about with a book under his arm, as happy as a king . . .'

When he returned to work, Bravo wrote regularly to Florence, letters that were both warm and amusing. She jokingly complained that his words were 'cold and undemonstrative', and that he wrote 'tersely, as all barristers do.' But that does not seem to have been the case – indeed, his letters provide an example of the considerable charm that had first attracted her. 'I walked up and down the road for half an hour,' he wrote, 'waiting for a letter from you, and the postman came whistling along, the lighthearted wretch, though he had no letter for me . . . I am as perfectly happy as I can be in your absence . . . I am always thinking of you and longing for you, and I have your little dog beside me at the fire. So much do I love you that I derive some comfort from the society of the little animal which you like . . . I wish I could sleep away my life until you return.'

In due course, at the end of October, Bravo proposed.

*

So it had happened. Florence told her sister that Bravo had professed his love for her, and that he had been thinking for some time that he should marry. But Florence's position at this moment was very different from that of most young widows being courted by eligible bachelors. She wanted to accept Bravo's proposal. She wanted to get married again and put the scandals of the past behind her. But there were two serious obstacles to doing so. First, there was James Gully. He was no longer her lover, true, but he still regarded himself as her fiancé. They continued with their walks and their dinners, and Florence had returned his pledges of love. She hesitated at the thought of betraying him after everything he had done for her.

Then there was the much more serious issue of her reputation, and of its effect on Bravo. Florence knew that her neighbours in Balham would certainly disclose to the Bravo family all the lurid details of her affair with Dr Gully once they read about her engagement in the newspapers. Yet if she confessed now, and told Charles everything, she was certain she would lose him.

Florence's approach to these problems provides us with a useful insight into her nature. First, she tackled James Gully. Instead of disposing of him personally, face to face, she adjourned to a house in Brighton and wrote to him. The letter was long and rambling. She didn't mention Bravo. Instead she invented a family illness as an excuse for ending their relationship (both her parents, it will be remembered, had alienated her because of her affair). Gully was 'devastated' when he received the letter, and telegraphed the hotel to say that he was on his way down to see her. Florence persuaded Mrs Cox to receive him at the station, to try to smooth things over. Later she met him in the dining room of the hotel and she stuck to her story. 'She told me that her mother was ill and that she desperately wanted to see her,' recalled Gully. 'She told me that she had written to her family confirming that we had broken off our friendship.'

But as they were leaving the hotel, Gully managed to extract the truth. 'As we were parting, she admitted to me that she was being "approached" by a man called Charles Bravo,' he said. 'She told me that her friendship with him was a very serious one, and that she anticipated a marriage proposal from him. I implored her to at least wait before she accepted any proposal, and to be properly acquainted with Mr Bravo. This she agreed to do.'

There can be no doubt that Gully initially believed that Florence would not go ahead with her marriage, and that she would eventually come back to him if he bided his time. He was encouraged by her willingness to listen to his advice. He was encouraged, he said, by the fact that she put her hand across his after lunch, and by the way in which she looked at him as he climbed into his carriage. But such is the blindness of love. Florence was no longer the sickly and depressed girl who had come to him for help. She was an assured young woman, buoyed up by her status and wealth. And he no longer figured in her plans. The clues had been there, scattered at every encounter, but the old man had not seen them: he had always hated Florence using cosmetics, but she had started doing so in recent months, darkly painting her lips and eyelashes. He disliked women who dyed their hair. And Florence had twice come back from the salon with a flaming-red tint. Each week she had seemed to dress more flamboyantly than the last, gradually exchanging the laced embroidery of Collard's for dresses that were tighter, bolder, that moulded her body into provocative contours. It was all indicative of the new sexual confidence that Gully himself had generated.

Sure enough, a month after the meeting in Brighton, the doctor received a letter from Mrs Cox. It was a bombshell. There was a dreadful simplicity to it, he later recalled – merely the date, the time, the location of the church. Gully lit a fire and burned the letter. He went to the study and sat down to write a reply, a 'very angry letter', full of violent reproach. He called the butler into the room and asked him to deliver it at once, adding that if Florence or Mrs Cox ever appeared at his house they were to be turned away at the door. But even in the passion of his own anger Gully seems to have discovered that he could not be cruel. No sooner had the butler returned from the Priory than he sent him back again, bearing a second letter, full of apology, expressing good wishes. Eight months later his mixed reactions were explored in court:

Q: Let me ask you this: at that interview [in Brighton] did you not tell Mrs Ricardo that you would die?

A: – That I would die?

Q: If she left you?

A: No – nothing of the kind – not even in a poetic flight. (Laughter in court.) I told her that I would be very unhappy for a while.

A: Did you tell her that you would never see her again?

Q: I did not say that I would not see her again – it was the other way around: she said that she would not see me. I was at that time much attached to her, and I was under the impression that she was much attached to me.

By now Florence's mind had turned to other matters. She barely noticed the communications coming from Orwell Lodge. She had disposed of Gully and the matter was closed. She was now much more preoccupied with her second problem. How could she disclose her past without frightening Charles away? How could she explain? How could she make the words sound like anything except what they really were – a series of embarrassed excuses?

She decided to start by manufacturing the sudden distress that had always stood her in such good stead in the past. She invited Charles to dinner and halfway through the meal she broke down. Charles leapt up to soothe her. He pressed her for an explanation. But she would not give it. She waited for him to coax it from her. He gave her a glass of burgundy and sat with her, holding her hand. And eventually she gave up the ruinous secret, wrapped neatly in tears and remorse. 'I told him that I had become acquainted with Dr Gully after the failure of my marriage,' she said. 'I told him that I had been constantly in Dr Gully's company. I told him we had gone together to Kissingen and that I had become pregnant. I told him everything.' When the whole story had come out Florence got up and left the room. 'I left him alone to make a decision,' she said.

She went into the study and paced up and down for twenty minutes. When she returned, he was standing by the window, his back to her. He said: 'I am grateful that you told me. I have given it careful thought. I still want you to be my wife. We all make mistakes. But of course you must never see Dr Gully again.' Later that night he said to Mrs Cox: 'She has told me about her past. But I think that a woman who has gone wrong once is likely to be all the more careful afterwards.'

The next day Bravo was gracious enough to put the relationship back on an even footing. 'He told me that he had been thinking about Dr Gully,' Florence said, 'and that it was time to tell me that he had also had an illicit affair. He said that he had kept a woman in Maidenhead for five years, together with her child. I said I was glad he had confessed. After he had said that, we made an agreement: I would never mention this woman, and he would never mention the name of Dr Gully. All was forgotten.'

Charles Bravo's reaction to Florence's confession should make us pause for a moment. Florence's mother later alleged that Charles Bravo had 'a money mania', that he was obsessed by the power of money, by the need to conserve it, by the ruthlessness necessary to acquire it. Florence herself accused him of 'greed and penury'. 'In fact his meanness disgusted me,' she said. His stockbroker said: 'He always took a very keen interest in money matters. He was worried by losses.'

It is dangerous to generalize about Victorian moral codes. But it is almost certain that no man of Charles Bravo's background would consider marrying a woman who had just confessed to aborting a pregnancy during an adulterous affair with a sixty-seven-year-old man unless he was chiefly interested in her money. Certainly, during the Coroner's inquest, Joseph Bravo's solicitor would go to great lengths to try to prove that Charles had not been aware of Florence's affair when he married her. To have married her when her adultery had been exposed was, in the public perception, the action of a fortune-hunter.

And there were other clues to his motives. Shortly before the wedding, Florence decided to invoke her right to keep her fortune after her marriage. Up until 1870 the law had entitled a husband to assume all the assets of his new wife. Anything that she had acquired through the death of her parents or of an earlier husband was automatically transferred to him. This was a situation that had provoked increasing criticism in an age when women were gradually liberating themselves from traditional roles rooted in submission and dependence. In 1870, therefore, the law had been changed. Women were allowed to keep whatever assets they brought into marriage, provided a legal settlement confirming their intention to do this had been ratified in court before the marriage took place. Florence Ricardo was the last woman on earth to go along with the old convention. So she contacted her solicitor. When he was told of her plans, however, Charles Bravo informed Florence that he would not marry her. 'I cannot contemplate a marriage,' he said, 'that does not make me master in my own house. I cannot sit upon a chair or eat from a table which does not belong to me.' Bravo wrote to Robert Campbell and urged him to intervene on his behalf (which Campbell did). He also visited Florence's solicitor for the same purpose. The solicitor said that when Bravo called on him, and he offered him his congratulations on the forthcoming marriage, Bravo replied: 'Damn your congratulations – I've come about the money!'

For a moment it seemed as if the wedding was off. 'It appeared to me that he was marrying me for my money,' Florence said. In due course, however, a compromise was agreed. Florence would give Charles the lease of the Priory and all the furnishings. She would also make a will in his favour. In return she would retain control of her fortune.

But if Bravo's motives were purely financial, then Florence's motives were, in a sense, no less mercenary. She wanted back her respectability. Her rejection of her old lover and her liaison with Bravo was never an affair of the heart – it was simply a response to sociological pressures. 'I had not in the least grown tired of his company,' Florence said later, of Gully. 'No one could grow tired of him. He is so clever.' But the affair had ejected Florence from a traditional world of middle-class norms and routines, which she now wished to reinhabit. After four years in the wilderness, socially marginalized, she wanted to restore her position.

And so, on 7 December 1875, at eleven in the morning, Charles and Florence were married at All Saints Church, Kensington.

Charles Bravo had less than five months to live.

CHAPTER THREE

The Mistress of the House

Here at the Priory I am so thoroughly at home that it almost
seems as if I have never lived anywhere else.
CHARLES BRAVO, 12 January 1876

Marriage has teeth.
West Indian proverb

Charles Bravo's marriage to Florence had repercussions that
extended beyond the lives of the newly-weds. The marriage would
also affect the lives and livelihoods of more than a dozen people:
Mrs Cox and her three boys; Bravo's mistress in Maidenhead, and
the child who depended upon him financially; Dr Gully; the seven
members of staff at the Priory. This was a marriage that was
destined to create casualties.

There was, for instance, Dr Gully. Gully was making plans to go
away for a while, back to Austria, to resume his research. But he
was still brooding over Florence. He and his butler, Pritchard, had
watched the wedding procession going up Streatham Hill, peering
through the windows of Orwell Lodge. At that moment Gully knew
that he had lost his mistress for good. There could be no hope of the
reconciliation that he had once dreamt of.

Gully had given up everything for Florence: his home; his social
position; his circle of friends in Malvern; his relationship with his
two sisters (who had managed his household after the break-up of
his marriage). He, too, had been the victim of the same local gossip
that had driven Florence to seek a respectable marriage – and in his

case there had been an eminent professional reputation to be tarnished as well. But he had been prepared to pay that price. He had twice told Florence that he was willing to endure social ostracism in order to continue his relationship with the woman he loved. It was no wonder that Florence's marriage left him feeling bitter. According to his butler, Gully considered himself 'properly tricked'. 'He said that Mrs Ricardo had treated him extremely badly,' Pritchard added. Pritchard also said that Dr Gully had given him 'strict instructions' not to admit Mrs Bravo into the house.

Later, Mrs Cox was asked in court about Dr Gully's emotional state at the time of Florence's marriage to Charles:

Q: Was it your impression that Dr Gully was deeply hurt by Mrs Bravo's rejection of him?

A: Dr Gully was much displeased when Mrs Ricardo broke off the attachment.

Q: I believe you saw Dr Gully in Brighton with Mrs Ricardo –

A: Yes.

Q: – at the interview when she told him the relationship was over?

A: Yes.

Q: And how did he seem?

A: He was distressed.

Q: Heartbroken?

A: I think heartbroken is too strong. He was a man of enormous dignity. But it was clear that he was hurt.

Was Dr Gully's pain and anger focused solely on Florence? Or did he believe that she had been as much a victim in the matter as himself – a victim of Charles Bravo's mercenary charms?

Certainly, Bravo himself was wary of Gully's decision to remain in the neighbourhood. Shortly after the wedding Bravo received an anonymous letter, accusing him of marrying Florence for her money. Bravo called the letter 'vile'. He showed it to Mrs Cox, who advised him to burn it. He told her that he was sure that the letter came from Gully. 'He called Dr Gully the "old wretch",' said Florence, 'and said that it was "very wicked of him to send such a thing".' A second letter arrived a fortnight later. A third came just after Christmas. Bravo began to feel that he was the victim of a vendetta. Although the letters made no direct threats, and although their real author was never conclusively identified, they provided an uncomfortable reminder that someone connected to the couple bore Charles Bravo a real grudge.

Another domestic servant whose life was disrupted by the arrival of Charles Bravo was Florence's coachman, George Griffiths. Griffiths had been with Florence for four years, and lived quietly in the grounds of the Priory.

Two weeks before the wedding, Bravo had called Griffiths into the study and sacked him. 'Mr Bravo said that he was dismissing me because of an accident that had happened in Bond Street,' Griffiths recalled. 'I was driving Mrs Bravo and I ran into a wine cart. Mr Bravo said it was my fault and gave me my notice.'

The exchange had left Griffiths incandescent with rage. His wife was pregnant, he insisted. They had nowhere else to go. But Bravo was implacable. He would evict Griffiths from the cottage within a fortnight, he said. Griffiths complained bitterly to other members of staff. 'He was very angry and upset,' recalled Mrs Cox. 'He was very bitter,' said the butler. 'He couldn't seem to shake it off.'

George Griffiths found new employment in Kent, at a house in Herne Bay. But he didn't leave Balham without a parting shot – an exchange that was to intrigue people after Charles Bravo's death. One morning Griffiths had found himself in the bar of the local hotel, the Bedford. He had already consumed a considerable amount of alcohol, and was still smarting at the recent turn of events. When Bravo's name was mentioned by the landlord, Griffiths became suddenly fiery. 'He started cursing Mr Bravo,' said the manager of the hotel, 'saying that Mr Bravo had sacked him. He said: "I'd still be there now if it wasn't for him." He seemed very put out at what had happened.' The manager added: 'As he was leaving he looked at me and said something strange. He said that Mr Bravo would get what was coming to him, and that his days were numbered. I was very shocked at first. But then I just thought it was the spleen of the man, that he was angry at being sacked.'

'What were his exact words?' the manager was asked, in court.

'He said he wouldn't want to be in Mr Bravo's shoes,' came the reply. 'He said Mr Bravo would get what was coming to him. He said that Mr Bravo would be dead in a few months.'

It should have been the start of a new life for Florence. Of course she was still tied to the Priory, with all its memories of Dr Gully; there he was, less than a hundred yards away, ambling up and down Balham High Street, like Banquo's ghost. And she was still a tainted woman – even within her own family there were people who couldn't overlook her past. But she had begun again. She had survived an abortion and a scandalous affair and had married an eminently eligible bachelor – rich, educated and ambitious. 'We felt it was a new beginning,' said Mrs Cox, later. And Florence was optimistic, too: 'My past has been a very sad one,' she wrote, 'but it will now be for ever blotted out and forgotten.'

After a short honeymoon in Brighton the newly-weds returned to London and began to settle down to domestic life. Bravo wrote daily to his wife whenever he was away at Sessions, his letters full of romantic, carolling touches. 'Apart from the beginning of my first marriage,' Florence said, 'this was the happiest time of my life.'

Slowly, Florence found local society opening up to her. She planned a fabulous party for Christmas, inviting thirty-one guests, including the Mayor of Streatham. 'There has been a great slaughter for the feast,' Bravo wrote, 'hens, pheasants and chicken. I wanted to have a gander on the table, surrounded by his wives, but Florence wouldn't hear of it.' Bravo's partner, Edward Hope, stayed the night, along with four others, and had an opportunity to observe whether married life suited his old friend. 'I saw them at dinner and again the next day, when we played tennis,' he recalled. 'Charles showed me around the estate, the gardens and stables. He seemed very pleased with everything. He was very proud of his wife and very proud of the Priory. He seemed to be remarkably happy.'

Florence's parents, too, were pleased that their daughter had finally gained respectability. She took the opportunity that Christmas to apologize to her father for 'the pain' she had caused him 'with regard to the last sad years of separation'. 'Believe me when I say how sorry I am,' she added.

The Campbells' satisfaction at the new marriage was heightened by a telegram, received at Buscot on 9 January, announcing that Florence was pregnant. Dr Harrison from Streatham had attended her and confirmed it. The baby was due in the autumn and Charles felt certain it was going to be a boy. He and Florence had already spent a happy afternoon discussing names for the baby. Bravo was determined that it should be Charles – 'Charles the Second', he joked. It seemed at last as though Florence had found the stability that had eluded her for so long.

Within three months, however, things had dramatically changed; Florence had once again returned to Buscot, seeking sanctuary. Once again she brought back stories of domestic abuse and an intolerable marriage; once again she was determined never to spend another night with her husband.

In spite of the general optimism – founded more in relief than common sense – it had in fact been a problematic situation from the start. At the heart of the new marriage was an unresolved question about the psychological control of their relationship, and about the structure of power within it.

For Charles, there was nothing more natural than that he be able to walk into the Priory and govern it from the outset. He expected his wife to obey his wishes. 'I cannot contemplate a marriage,' he had once said, 'that does not make me master in my own house.' Bravo did not expect obedience simply because his wife had pledged it in her vows. He was not religious. He expected it for a far more prosaic reason: she was a woman and he was a man. Masculinity, in fact, was the essence of his power: it was men who governed in public life, who managed the great professions, who ran commerce and trade, who conducted war, who pushed back the frontiers of science and technology. Similarly, it was men who commanded the household and the family – disciplined the children and directed the wife. The role of the female entailed nothing more than the cultivation of an environment conducive to her husband's success in the world. Not every man in Victorian England agreed with this, of course. 'The status of women in our society,' wrote John Stuart Mill, in the year that Charles Bravo turned twenty-one, 'is worse than that of slaves in many countries.' But Mill's voice was a besieged one, popularly rejected by its own radicalism. It was Bravo's view that prevailed in contemporary culture. For such men – men who lived and traded on the past – women were a little like pet animals; they required kindness and pain in equal doses, leavened with the brisk command of their natural masters. For a wife to resist her husband's will at any point was both a challenge to the ruling law – and an act of emasculation.

Most women would have accepted this with a cool ambiguity. It was a view into which they had been socialized by their parents and by the world around them. They did not publicly question it.

But Florence was no ordinary woman. Subjugation was no longer an issue with her. Florence had already suffered greatly at the hands of her 'natural superiors', during her first marriage, and she had abandoned any sense of deference to them. From the moment she walked out on Alexander, she failed to believe in the legitimacy of a social system that compelled obedience to a man simply because of his sex. She had lost confidence in the prevailing ethos. And the inheritance of a large personal fortune had merely augmented this view. The days when a man dictated to her how she lived her life were gone. She would do as she pleased. She certainly would not be told how to conduct her affairs in a household where she 'found the money for things'.

As a sensible woman, Florence would have known that this attitude would cause problems. It was a self-conscious expression of defiance. It would have tried the patience of a man of modern sentiment. But she had confidently imagined that she and Bravo would be able to compromise. During their courtship she had come to believe that he was a civilized person. 'I will ever have a great regard for you,' she had written, 'for I think you are a very good man.' Now she was to learn how badly she had misjudged things.

The first example of this conflict was in itself quite trivial. Florence had come down to breakfast one morning in the New Year to find her husband swamped by paperwork. He had decided to take over the management of the house, he said. He then told Florence that she lived far too extravagantly and that he needed to curb her expenditure. He would start by dismissing her maid, Fanny Plascott, and transferring her duties to the housemaid, Mary Ann Keeber. Then he would let one of the gardeners go. He also told Florence that he wished to landscape the flower beds, so that a second gardener could be dismissed. Later they could talk about selling the horses.

Florence had anticipated this and met it head on. 'I told him that he had no right to interfere in my arrangements,' she said. 'I told him that I had always been used to having a lady's maid, ever since I was a child. I told him that my garden was one of my greatest pleasures.' She added: 'I reminded him that I had always lived within my means – and I was accustomed to looking after my own affairs.'

Florence may have anticipated a reaction, but she had completely underestimated its severity. During the exchange that followed she witnessed for the first time the fury of her new husband's temper. It was a side to his character that she hadn't known existed. 'He had been so charming to me up until that point,' she recalled. 'I had not expected him to be so *passionate*.' Bravo paced the room. He clutched a copy of Florence's accounts and waved them under her nose. At one point he slammed his fist on the table so loudly that a cup and saucer fell onto the floor. He reminded his wife that he was head of the household. The marriage had made him so. It was his will that had to prevail. 'Whenever I challenged him,' she said, 'he became very agitated.'

The scene ended with Bravo leaving the room 'in a blind fury'. He did not speak to his wife for the rest of the day. In the evening an uneasy truce settled on the Priory. The subject of 'retrenchment' was not mentioned. They went to bed exchanging monosyllables.

But over the coming weeks there were further arguments between them, again of a domestic nature, as Bravo tried to assert control of the relationship. Florence realized that the lengths to which her new husband could be pushed were much shorter than she had first thought. 'He was short-tempered to the last degree,' she recalled. 'His temper was impossible.'

On one occasion Bravo insisted that Florence cancel an order for peat which she had placed in the village. 'If this is what gardening costs,' he said, 'we must give it up.' When she refused to do so he 'began to attack me for my spending, saying that I would make him bankrupt.' On another occasion they clashed over the horses. 'If we put down the horses we can save four hundred a year,' Bravo said. But when Florence refused he 'became very angry and aggressive'.

'It did not take much to upset him,' said Mrs Cox, who witnessed many of these scenes. 'I remember an occasion when there was a quarrel between them and he was very violent. He said he would go. This was about ten or eleven at night. He unbarred the front door and went down the drive. All this was over a letter . . . On another occasion he got annoyed with Mrs Bravo for lying down. She asked him to leave the room so she could rest. He threw an awful tantrum about it. He said she shouldn't have asked him to leave the room and that she didn't love him any more. He said he despised himself for marrying her, that she was "a selfish pig". He then said that he was going to leave. He went to fetch his coat. I said to him: "What do you think will become of Florence if you go away?"

'He said: "Let her go back to Gully."

'I told him that it was very wrong of him.'

Bravo's threats to leave were a measure of how seriously he viewed the struggle between them. Florence seemed prepared to tough out his reaction – she, after all, had the cheque book. But Bravo was not the kind of man who capitulated easily. If he could not gain control of the household *directly*, he would find other ways in which he could break his wife's resistance. There was no more obvious outlet for his frustration than in the bedroom.

In the New Year, five weeks after their wedding, Florence went to Brighton to see Dr Charles Dill, the physician who had treated her throughout her first marriage. According to Dr Dill, Florence made 'grave charges' against her husband over their sexual relationship, claiming that he 'engaged in a persistent line of conduct'. The conduct, it was convincingly alleged, was anal intercourse. Florence was powerless to resist her husband, and the intercourse was having a shattering effect on her delicate mental stability.

Anal intercourse was actually fairly common in the nineteenth century, particularly amongst married couples who didn't use contraception. For Bravo it would probably have been a routine part of a healthy sex life. He was much more sexually permissive than his wife, having kept a mistress for some years, and having been a frequent visitor to Paris, regarded by the English as a place of unspeakable debauchery. Yet in the climate of the Priory anal penetration became something much more sinister than merely the gratification of Charles Bravo's animal impulses. Anal sex was an instrument of punishment and subjugation; a degrading attack on Florence's modesty; a fundamental assault on her inalienable right to determine what happened to her own body.

All her adult life Florence had placed great importance on her ability to manage the sexual activity in her relationships. She didn't become pregnant during her years with Alexander because she didn't want to bring children into a crumbling marriage. So she must have controlled very firmly the times when she allowed Alexander near her. She had shown a similar resolve when she was sleeping with James Gully. *She* had decided exactly when their relationship became sexual. And she had had no hesitation in banishing him from her bed when the abortion went wrong. She was a woman who regarded the ability to dictate both the form and the timing of sexual contact to be her absolute right. Now, in the face of her repeated protests, Bravo snatched that right from her. His assaults not did not merely violate her identity as a woman. They served to remind her that not a shred of the autonomy that she had exercised in her previous relationships applied any longer.

Angered by his behaviour, and too weary to fight back, Florence did what she had done in the past: she retreated to Buscot, seeking parental protection and the opportunity to think.

She arrived at Buscot 'very distressed', pouring out the recent train of events. She told her parents that Charles had 'violent ebullitions of temper', that he sought 'constant retrenchment' and that his 'meanness disgusted her'. 'My daughter didn't see why she couldn't manage her household as she liked,' said Mrs Campbell. Florence did not mention the sexual proclivities of her husband – 'it is not the sort of thing I would wish to discuss with any man,' she remarked at the inquest, 'except a doctor' – but she did recount the various occasions when they had rowed: the time in the morning room when Bravo had slammed his fist down on the table; how he had twice threatened to leave her and had stormed from the house, coming back only under the coaxing of Mrs Cox. She recalled how he had taken to opening her mail – even scrutinizing the letters addressed to the servants. She explained how Bravo threw 'tantrums' when she was short with him; how he snatched up her wine glass when he thought she had had enough; sat smoking his pipe in her bedroom when she was ill. The grievances poured out. And there was something else. In the last few weeks, she claimed, Charles had developed a growing obsession with James Gully. The 'obsession' had been started by some anonymous letters: two during the Christmas period; one in the New Year; all in the same hand. The letters had unsettled him. They accused him of marrying Florence for her money and were 'very unpleasant'.

'If you had not told me about Dr Gully before our marriage,' he had said to Florence, after the first letter had arrived, 'I would have been on the sea tonight.'

At one point Bravo had shown the letters to Mrs Cox and demanded: 'Is this Dr Gully's handwriting?' Mrs Cox had said no, she thought not. But Bravo had already made up his mind. Dr Gully was the author. 'He calls Dr Gully an old wretch,' Florence told her father. 'He says he will not be happy until he sees his coffin going across Tooting Common.'

Later Florence said: 'My husband had promised not to mention Dr Gully's name before our marriage. Yet now he was constantly speaking of him. He was always abusing him, calling him "that wretch", and attacking me for my former acquaintance with him.' Florence recalled how, seeing her off at Balham railway station just after their honeymoon, Bravo had asked: 'Is Dr Gully going to Buscot as well?' On another occasion, riding into town, their carriage had passed Gully's house and Charles had taunted her: 'Did you see anybody?' When she had reprimanded him – 'I'm not always talking about your other woman' – his face had grown dark. 'He looked at me in a very determined way and I became frightened,' she said. 'He looked as if he was going to do something violent.'

Robert Campbell probably felt a weary exasperation at his daughter's apparent inability to get along with any man she chose to live with. But her mother was more circumspect. She had had her own doubts about Bravo: his 'money mania', his 'cruelty'. She remembered an incident when she had challenged him herself during a conversation and his face had turned 'white and livid'. She remembered, too, how jealous he had seemed of Dr Gully, 'saying that he wished he could "annihilate" him'. She had in fact unsuccessfully urged Florence to delay her wedding, to wait until the spring, to be 'better acquainted' with her fiancé.

The Campbells agreed to let Florence remain at Buscot for a short period. They were setting out for a holiday in Italy and she could have the run of the house while they were gone. Her sister, Edith, came to stay, too, and her brother, William.

While she was there, the first of a series of letters arrived for her from the Priory. Bravo appeared to have been shaken by his wife's desertion, and he wrote touchingly, imploring her to return. 'I miss you dreadfully, my darling wife,' he said. 'If you come back I will so take care of you that you will never leave me again.' Another began: 'Looking back on our ten weeks of marriage, I feel that many of my words to you, though kindly meant, were unnecessarily harsh. In

future my rebukes . . . shall be given with the utmost gentleness . . .'
Later he added: 'I only want your love. Without your love, honour
and riches are nothing.' A third letter started: 'In future, you will find
me to be the best of husbands. I long for you. My only object is to
make you happy.' He finished with a promise: 'I will always try to
please you – and to justify your choice of me as a husband.'

The problem with these letters from Florence's point of view was
that they did not admit error; nor did they pledge reform. They
merely attempted to warm the climate. There was no concession to
Florence's rights as his wife. She knew that if she returned to the
Priory, having strung out her silence for as long as she could, it
would be to engage in a reconciliation on terms that had already
failed. But what other options were there? She was two months
pregnant. She had nowhere else to go. Florence had come to Buscot
to make a decision; but circumstances had already made it for her.

CHAPTER FOUR

'An Extremely Dangerous Woman'

He was so accustomed to be being waited upon, that he did
not know what it was to wait upon a lady.
                    FLORENCE BRAVO, 15 May 1876

I have felt a change coming over her for some time. She does
not care for me any longer.
                    CHARLES BRAVO, 3 April 1876

Snow slanted across London and the winter deepened. At the Priory,
Charles had been left to brood on the behaviour that had driven away
his bride of less than two months. Yet he refused to admit a role in
her desertion. Although he adopted a remorseful tone in his letters,
he told a member of staff that Florence was 'a selfish pig'. She had
been spoilt all her life – by her father and mother, by her lover, by
herself. He was not to blame for her 'selfishness'. He had stood up to
her, as any husband should.

Instead of worrying, Bravo seized the opportunity presented by
Florence's absence to execute some of the domestic changes he
wanted. At the centre of them were his new plans for Mrs Cox. She,
like the coachman George Griffiths, was about to become another
casualty of the new marriage.

Bravo had been considering Mrs Cox's position for a long time,
ever since he had first toyed with the idea of marriage. And his
feelings had grown less and less ambiguous. 'I saw him one morning
with his pen in his hand, sitting at his desk, calculating something,'
said his friend, Edward Hope. 'I asked him what he was doing and he

said he was adding up the household expenses. He was always concerned with such matters. He remarked on how expensive it was to keep a woman, the clothes they always wanted. Then he said that he was thinking of dismissing Mrs Cox, because she was costing him a great deal of money. He said: "After all, she must be costing us three hundred a year."'

Bravo's feelings towards Mrs Cox were governed partly by self-interest and partly by jealousy. She was costing them money. She worked hard, of course. But there was nothing that she did that couldn't be done by other members of staff. Joseph Bravo recalled: 'He was anxious that Mrs Cox should leave. She was an expense on the household and had no particular duties.'

But this was not the whole story. There were, of course, more subtle reasons for Bravo's decision. He couldn't fail to sense how close his wife was to her companion. Jane had been at Florence's side through all the most traumatic moments of recent years. She had become a repository for her mistress's deepest secrets, as well as a valued source of advice and support – all the things, in short, that were now part of Bravo's role as a husband. If Florence was worried she went to see Jane; if she wanted to make plans she went to see Jane; if she needed to share a confidence she went to see Jane. How many times had he walked into a room in which the two women were chatting only to find a sudden silence descend upon them as he entered? The friendship between them amounted to a virtual conspiracy.

It is clear that Bravo sensed the irony in his plans. Mrs Cox had brought them together. There would have been no marriage without her. 'I owe her something,' he had told Hope, 'because she used to urge my suit.' But such sentiment counted for little. In the final analysis it was only the implementation of his will that mattered. 'He was a man of very little sentiment,' Hope remarked.

Yet as he deliberated on exactly how to get rid of the companion, something made Bravo feel curiously cautious, even uneasy. He told his stepfather that he thought Mrs Cox was a strange and secretive woman. And he had the feeling that, once crossed, she would make a most formidable enemy.

One evening Bravo called Mrs Cox into the study and told her that he was dismissing her. He appreciated that she had obligations; she had her boys to consider, their education and upkeep, and her own circumstances. So he would give her plenty of time to find a new position. But she should not be in any doubt that he was dispensing with her services.

Mrs Cox must have been shattered by this news. She had never been happier than she was at the Priory. And it was not merely the practical benefits. In the last two years she had come to see Florence as a daughter; a wilful girl, sometimes astonishingly naive, but with a great deal of charm and beauty. (Her own daughter Sarah had died in infancy, claimed by the same consumption that had killed her husband.) 'Charles told me that I was "a good little woman",' she said later. 'He said that I loved Florence and that I always did the best I could for him. And it was true.'

But it was not just the loss of Florence's friendship that worried the faithful companion. It was Charles Bravo's economizing that would produce ruin. Mrs Cox had no home of her own. Prior to joining Florence she had been lodging in a single room with a Miss Child, in a miserable bedsit in Streatham. Furthermore, she owed money on her mortgage and had many private debts. In 1868 she had founded a ladies' seminary in Suffolk and the school had collapsed, leaving her owing money that she was still struggling to pay back. She had just purchased enough votes to secure her youngest son's entry into the same private school where his two brothers were being educated – St Anne's Asylum for the Children of Distressed Gentlefolk. But she had only managed it by borrowing almost a year's worth of salary – £81, which she was repaying in fractional instalments. All in all, Bravo's plans attacked Jane Cox at the most fundamental level, and threatened her capabilities as a mother. Worse still was the knowledge that she could no longer count on Florence's support. There had been disputes over the domestic arrangements already, bitter arguments that Florence lost more frequently than she won. Although Florence, on her return from Buscot, confirmed that she would resist Bravo's efforts to dismiss her companion, Mrs Cox was sceptical: Florence had vowed to protect Rance, the gardener, a month earlier – and had watched helpless as Bravo ordered him from the estate. Mrs Cox knew that her mistress's ability to defy her husband had been gravely weakened by his driving persistence and his foul temper.

Yet Jane Cox was a remarkable woman. Bravo was right to have hesitated. The great criminal lawyer, Sir Douglas Strait, said later that he had never seen such a formidable woman in all his years at the Bar. She had not raised three boys single-handedly without mining the resourcefulness that was necessary for survival. She was shrewd and calculating; apparently submissive, but actually possessing an inflexible strength of character. 'Mrs Cox was a clever woman,' said Sir George Lewis, the Bravo family's solicitor. 'And – like many clever women – she was extremely dangerous when crossed.'

All marriages require a degree of luck in order to flourish. And Florence and Charles seemed to enjoy less than their fair share: the anonymous letters; the shadow of James Gully on their doorstep; the local gossip. Now things were to be complicated by more misfortune. Four days after her return from Buscot, just as relations between her and her husband seemed to be improving, Florence woke to find the sheets of her bed spotted with blood. Dr Harrison from Streatham was summoned, and immediately confirmed that she had miscarried her pregnancy. There was nothing for her to do, he said, except take plenty of rest.

When Bravo returned home later that day he was met on the stairs by Mrs Cox, who broke the news to him. Bravo hurried up to the bedroom and found Florence dozing. The doctor had administered a sedative. When she awoke they discussed the probable causes of the miscarriage. Bravo could think of nothing – she ate and slept properly; she had given up horse-riding and gardening.

During the course of their discussion Florence asked Charles if he would mind vacating the bedroom for a few days, so that Mrs Cox could sleep with her. She felt extremely debilitated, she said, and might need nursing through the night. Reluctantly, Bravo agreed. He moved his belongings out of the master bedroom and across the landing, to the little spare room at the front of the house.

The loss of the pregnancy, in a stronger marriage, might not have been a serious development. But here it presented another opportunity for Florence to see how little her husband really understood her, and how inappropriate his response to her needs really was.

The attitude of women towards miscarriages varies. Some are deeply traumatized by them; a few regard them with clinical detachment. We do not really know how Florence viewed her own – in keeping with the secrecy of her society she does not write openly about her feelings. But the evidence is there, nonetheless. She writes in some detail about the physical effects. The doctor, she said, had described her as 'unusually weak', and had ordered her to remain in bed for several days. 'I eat more than I did,' she wrote, 'but I am weak. It will be some time before I am able to get about as usual.' She talked of how she was trying to 'woo back sleep, one of the most important steps to recovery'. She added that Mary Ann had been 'very good' and that Mrs Cox had been 'all kindness to me'. 'I don't know what I should do without her,' she said.

Mrs Cox, meanwhile, gives us an insight into the psychological effects on Florence. She reports that Florence sank into a depression, that she was unable to sit up in bed, to take food, to express any interest in things. Mrs Cox said that she tried to persuade Florence to spend an afternoon in the garden, finishing her designs for the orchard. But she retreated inside after only a few minutes, unable to face it. 'It seems ages before one starts to feel well again,' Florence wrote. 'It is a long business.'

In the light of this, Bravo's own reaction to what had happened was interesting. His attitude, put at its kindest, was dispassionate. His correspondence barely mentions Florence, merely the loss of his son. 'Florence is very weak,' he wrote. 'She lost Charles the Second on Thursday, a youth of great promise. The doctor said he had the Bravo countenance. He will tell you his other details when he sees you.' In another letter Bravo confirmed that his cousin, a surgeon, had visited Florence to check on her progress. Yet – while he describes in some detail his cousin's state of health, and talks about his own touches of rheumatism – he fails to write more than a line about the condition of his wife, depressed and bedridden for a week. For Bravo it was as if Florence had suffered little more than a heavy dose of the common cold.

Bravo's attitude was perhaps best exemplified by an argument that he provoked with his wife when she was finally back on her feet. Florence had decided to take a holiday in Worthing. 'The doctor had recommended a change of air,' she said. But Bravo was against the idea, principally 'on the grounds of expense'. During the course of the argument Bravo lost his temper and struck his wife in the face, knocking her to the ground. He then stormed out of the bedroom, went downstairs, fetched his coat, and began to march off down the drive. Mrs Cox, reaching him on the main road, managed to coax him back inside, but only after Bravo had again attacked Florence for her 'selfishness'.

Of course, Bravo's attitude was classically masculine; he failed to grasp the extent to which the miscarriage had affected his wife. He may even have blamed her, as many men do, for the loss of his child. At any rate, in an already tense atmosphere, a fresh cycle of recrimination could only make matters worse.

With Florence sick, and Charles slowly relieving her of her duties, Mrs Cox found that she had more and more time on her hands. Although she continued to busy herself with chores, half of them were of the Protestant kind – performed merely to keep her occupied.

One morning in early spring Mrs Cox took a train into London to do some shopping. What happened that morning was to be of considerable interest to the police, two months later. When she arrived at Balham railway station she noticed Dr Gully, studying the railway timetable. There was a flicker of embarrassment when their eyes met through the crowd. But then Gully smiled at her. 'He came across to me and asked me how I was,' Mrs Cox remembered. 'When the train arrived we agreed to share a carriage, as we were both going to Victoria.'

There was a certain inevitability to this meeting: Balham was a small place; both Dr Gully and Mrs Cox relied on the railways to make their trips into town. So it was unsurprising that the same thing happened again less than a fortnight later. This time Gully did mention Florence. 'He told me that he had lent Mrs Bravo a book of newspaper cuttings, about his life in Malvern. He said that Mrs Bravo still had the book and he wanted to give it to his granddaughter. I said that I would drop it in at his house.'

During the next six weeks, Mrs Cox and Dr Gully were seen together five times in public: on the Victoria train; outside shops and stores; in the street. They described their contact as 'cordial'. But it was clear that some degree of the old warmth between them was returning. Then, during their fifth meeting, an unusual development occurred. Mrs Cox mentioned Florence's recent miscarriage. She was unable to sleep, she said, and asked the doctor if he could prescribe anything.

Gully said that he would prepare some medication for her, made up principally of laurel water. He would not deliver it to the Priory – he would leave it at Mrs Cox's house in Notting Hill. Mrs Cox thanked him and then went on her way. Three days later a bottle duly arrived at Lancaster Road. One of her tenants signed for it. He noticed that it carried a small poison label. When Mrs Cox called the next day he gave her the bottle and gently inquired about the contents. He received an evasive reply.

This was not a sequence of events likely to produce an explanation from Mrs Cox. And it was made more suspicious by the fact that Florence never received any medicine from her companion. Mrs Cox never even mentioned her meetings with Dr Gully. Later, when the time came for the bottle to be produced, at the request of the police, Mrs Cox was unable to find it. 'The bottle appears to have vanished,' said a senior officer. 'Mrs Cox says she has thrown it away. She said that by the time she collected it Mrs Bravo had recovered and didn't need it.'

What was Dr Gully doing meeting a woman he had vowed never to speak to again? And what was Mrs Cox doing accepting a bottle from him; a bottle that carried a poison label?

'It seemed strange that Mrs Cox was receiving things from Dr Gully,' said Florence's mother. 'It would have been better if she hadn't done so.'

The spring was late in coming that year. *The Times* said that it had been a hard winter in south London, with many roads closed, and high drifts on the local commons at Streatham and Mitcham. But by mid-March the weather was improving. Florence – the miscarriage behind her – was busy designing a new strawberry bed, and replanting the kitchen garden. Her husband was away at Sessions a great deal, representing a client 'who was about as in the wrong as he could be'.

On or around 10 March, when they lunched together in London, Florence was told by her husband that the time had come for him to move back into the master bedroom. Her convalescence, he said, was over. It had been almost three weeks. She looked well enough. She was eating properly. It was time the household returned to normal life. Florence knew at once that this could mean only one thing. Bravo did not want to return to his wife's bed for reasons of emotional intimacy: nor merely for sexual gratification – he continued, after all, to engage her 'persistently' in anal intercourse, usually in the spare room. Her husband wanted to return to the bedroom because he felt it was time she became pregnant again.

For Florence, it was a moment she had dreaded. Of course it was only natural that her husband should want an heir. It was unrealistic to expect him to remain childless. But things were more complicated than that. Florence had been shocked by her own body's poor response to her miscarriage. She had been depressed and sick for the last three weeks. The thought of another pregnancy deeply unsettled her. What if she were unable to maintain it? What if it produced complications with her own health? Deep down, Florence doubted whether she would *ever* be able to give Charles the child he wanted; even whether, in trying to do so, she might kill herself.

The reason for Florence's fear was plain. It was not idle hypochondria. A few years earlier she had had a 'serious gynaecological illness'. Gully had attended her and described it as 'a want of action in the uterine organs'. A year later it had recurred. This time it was 'a suspension of the natural functions'. Florence remembered asking Gully whether the illness would affect her ability to conceive and he had said that he thought not. But then something disastrous had happened: Florence had had an abortion. The abortion had produced an infection; the infection had turned to septicaemia; the subsequent blood poisoning had almost killed her.

After the surgery, Florence had again wondered whether she would be able to conceive. Gully was sure that she would. But both of them knew that conception and delivery were two separate matters. The blood poisoning had almost certainly damaged Florence's womb, scarring the delicate tissue. This, coupled with the earlier illness, had stacked the deck against her. She might conceive easily enough – she seemed a remarkably fertile woman – but she would be lucky if she was able to carry the pregnancy to a full term.

And events had borne out her fear. Her pregnancy had been difficult and draining. It had ended unsuccessfully. Florence dreaded trying for another baby, and she knew that she was placing herself at risk if she did so. For this reason she had already resolved not to conceive again – at least not until she was back to full health.

The problem, of course, was Charles: impatient, callous, ruthless in pursuing what he wanted. He had already said that the best solution to a miscarriage was another pregnancy; and another if that was lost; and another. They simply had to go on, as many couples did, until they were successful. 'He was impossible when his mind was made up about something,' Florence told her father.

That afternoon Bravo moved his belongings back across the landing. Mrs Cox was ejected to her quarters, high on the top floor. After a good dinner, he and Florence retired to their marital bed. There he engaged his wife in sexual intercourse. Within a fortnight

Florence had telegraphed Buscot, sending shivers of unease through the house, to tell them that she was pregnant again.

Florence Bravo was not the first woman to marry a man who turned out to be someone else. But she was unusual in that she accomplished this feat twice. 'My husband could be very cruel,' she said. 'He was a very difficult man, and short-tempered to the last degree.' She was actually speaking about her second husband, but she could just have easily been referring to her first. The similarities were striking. Was it something in her psyche, this strange attraction to unsavoury men? Was she unconsciously seeking to punish herself, locked into a cycle of abuse? Or was she merely unlucky?

Soon after Florence had discovered she was pregnant, and soon after Mrs Cox had received her bottle of laurel water from James Gully, Charles Bravo was struck by a sudden and mysterious illness. He had risen at eight-thirty, as usual, and breakfasted with his wife in the dining room. Afterwards he had gone upstairs to collect his personal belongings. There he had begun to feel strangely nauseous. He called Rowe and asked him to bring up a glass of brandy. But when he came down the stairs ten minutes later, said the butler, he still looked 'very pale'. Against Rowe's advice, Bravo put on his hat and coat and set off for Balham railway station, a few minutes' walk down the road. A little way from the station he began to feel nauseous again, and sat on a wall, trying to settle his stomach. A moment or two later he was violently ill, vomiting into the gutter. He collected himself, decided to press on, and caught the 9.15 to Victoria. When the train arrived he took a cab across London, now feeling 'wretched', and arrived at his parents' house on Palace Green, where his mother immediately sent him to bed. She brought him a glass of curaçao and he dozed for an hour or so. When he came downstairs he felt 'weak' and looked 'trembly'. 'He was very pale,' said his stepfather. He walked from Palace Green into Kensington and then took a cab to Essex Court. 'He insisted on going to work,' said Joseph Bravo, 'against my advice.' By the end of the day, however, Bravo was feeling better. He returned to the Priory and consumed a large dinner. He even joked with Florence about the incident, saying that anyone who had seen him vomiting 'must have thought I had dined too well the night before'. But it was a strange episode, nonetheless. 'We were all concerned by it,' said Joseph Bravo. 'Charles had an excellent constitution. Nothing like this had ever happened to him before.'

CHAPTER FIVE

The Last Weekend

The manner of Mr Bravo's poisoning was so strange and inexplicable that it tempted the mind to fashion hypotheses which might provisionally account for it, and, in fact, the matter had the air of a problem in fiction rather than of a calamity in fact.

Daily News, 12 August 1876

By now it was Easter, and the Priory was once again alive with visitors. The long evenings had returned; the gardeners were busy building a melon pit for Florence, and three sets of strawberry beds. 'The flowers here are in great profusion,' Florence wrote, 'and so lovely.'

The household was busy with preparations for dinner guests; Florence's brother was visiting from Kingston, and a Mrs Fowke was coming from Norwood. Edward Hope, Bravo's partner at Essex Court, was also planning a visit, staying for two nights. But Florence did not attend the dinners. Although she received the guests, and took tea with them in the library, she complained constantly of feeling 'fragile', and chose on each occasion to retire early to bed.

The reason for Florence's fragility was simple: she had lost her second pregnancy a week earlier, exactly as she had feared. She had been in the garden this time, planning the spring flower beds, when she had been gripped by abdominal pain. Dr Harrison had attended her again and expressed alarm. The effects of a second miscarriage in two months were 'very serious indeed', according to her mother. Mrs Cox had begun another vigil, carrying trays of soup up to the bedroom, mixing iron tonics. Florence had again insisted that Charles move out of the bedroom and sleep across the landing. For the last week she and Mrs Cox had been sharing the big double bed. 'I am still poorly,' she wrote, 'and my back is very painful. We are intending to take a small furnished house at Worthing and to take the servants and carriages with us.'

Florence left her sick-bed on Easter Monday. It was a bright spring day, though everyone later complained of the east wind. She could hear Charles in the garden, playing with Mrs Cox's three boys. She tottered outside and sat on a deckchair, a rug on her lap. When it grew cold she went back inside and sat in the library, in front of the fire. She took a little supper on a tray and then, when Rowe came round lighting the gas lamps, she went up to bed.

The following morning – Tuesday, 18 April – everything seemed normal. 'There was no indication of what was about to happen,' said the butler, later. Florence woke early. She dressed and went downstairs. Mrs Cox was in the dining room, finishing her breakfast. She was rushing to catch the morning train to Worthing, where she was finding Florence a holiday house.

Charles and his wife left the Priory two hours later, planning to spend the day in town. They settled bills at the bank, visited the jewellers, and then parted at St James's Hall, in Piccadilly, where Charles was meeting Florence's uncle for lunch. Afterwards the two men went for a sauna at the Turkish baths in Jermyn Street. Then, at half past three, they walked along Mayfair, in the direction of Victoria, where Bravo was going to catch the 4.05 to Balham. On the way they met up with Bravo's friend, Frederick MacCalmont. Bravo urged MacCalmont to travel back to Balham with him and stay the night. But MacCalmont refused. He had business in town. 'If only I had accepted,' he said later, 'Charles might still be alive.' He did, however, accept Bravo's invitation of a game of tennis the following afternoon, and the three men parted company.

Florence had returned early when Bravo got back, and was lying down in the morning room. Bravo told her that he was taking one of the horses out and would be back within the hour. In the stables he asked the groom if the horses had been exercised. The groom replied that they did not need exercising 'since they had already been out to Clapham Junction'. 'I warned him not to take them,' he added. Bravo, however, elected to ignore the advice, and trotted off on Cremorne, saying that he would be back in twenty minutes. He reappeared nearly an hour later, shaking and sweating. The horse had bolted with him for four miles, he said, as far as Mitcham Common.

Bravo was helped off the horse and back into the house, spending the next hour in an armchair in the morning room, where Florence expressed alarm at his condition. 'He looked terrible,' she said. 'I had never seen him look so ill.' Bravo told her that he had 'come to grief on that wretched Cremorne'. Florence rang for a brandy. Half an hour went by and Bravo, overcome with exhaustion, seemed to fall asleep in his chair. When the butler put his head round the door he 'saw Mr Bravo sitting there, looking ill and wretched'.

At six-thirty Bravo decided that he needed a hot bath. But when he came to go upstairs he found that he couldn't even rise from his chair. 'He was so poorly,' said Florence, 'that I had to help him to his feet.' When they got to the stairs Bravo called for the butler. 'I helped him up to his room,' said Rowe. 'He was evidently in great pain, for he put his hands to his sides and cried out. He looked exceedingly pale – paler than he usually did, for he was generally pale. On the way up I asked him what had happened and he said that Cremorne had bolted with him. He had even lost his hat and had had to give a shilling to some labourers who had found it. I said: "I hope the horse didn't throw you, sir," and he smiled and said, "Oh no, Rowe, he didn't throw me." Afterwards, I helped him off with his boots.'

At seven-fifteen, Bravo dressed and went down for dinner. Just as he and Florence were preparing to eat, Mrs Cox returned from the coast, having found Florence a house to rent. She went upstairs, changed, and then reappeared in the dining room. According to the two women (and their account is largely substantiated by the staff serving dinner), the meal was a disaster. Indeed, it provided a colourful example of Charles Bravo at his most Victorian and disagreeable. He was sore from the horse-ride and a toothache had returned. During the meal he received a letter from his stepfather, chastising him for gambling on the stock market. He told Florence that his stepfather had 'no business' interfering in his affairs, and that he would write him 'a shirty letter'. When Mrs Cox gave him a photograph of the house she had rented for Florence he 'threw it down in disgust'.

After dinner the trio went into the morning room, where conversation was desultory. Bravo sat smoking his pipe. Florence felt 'too exhausted' to talk. After a little while the group gave up on the evening and decided to retire. Mrs Cox said to Florence: 'It's still early. Mary Ann will be having her dinner. I'll come up and help you undress.' The two women said goodnight to Charles and left. At the top of the stairs Florence paused and turned round. She asked Mrs Cox to 'be a dear' and get her 'a glass of marsala'. 'I'm so thirsty,' she added. She had just drunk a bottle of sherry at dinner.

Mrs Cox went back down to the dining room and opened the drinks cabinet. She poured half a glass of wine and went back upstairs, where Florence was now in her bedroom, undressing. After a moment the housemaid appeared with a bowl and a jug of warm water. She folded Florence's clothes and put them away in the dressing room, adjacent to the main bedroom. When she came back into the bedroom Florence, now in her nightgown, said: 'Bring me some wine will you, Mary Ann?'

Mary Ann takes up the story: 'I went downstairs and got some wine. As I was walking back along the hallway towards the stairs, Mr Bravo came out of the morning room. I knew he was going up to his room so I let him go before me. As he was going up he turned round and looked at me twice. He did not speak. I thought he was angry because he had always spoken before when he met me.'

Mary Ann was right: Bravo was angry. He had twice accused Florence of drinking too much during her illness. He had even spoken to Mrs Campbell on the subject. Florence had promised that she would cut down. But today she had consumed champagne at lunch, a bottle of sherry at dinner and now her second glass of marsala. Bravo went into her room. Speaking in French – conscious of Mary Ann's presence – he said: 'You have sent for more wine.' Florence didn't reply, but went on folding some clothes. Bravo then said that he would speak to her about the matter in the morning.

Mary Ann, meanwhile, tidied Florence's dressing room and then went back into her bedroom through a connecting door. Florence was in bed, apparently asleep. Mrs Cox was seated on a stool at the foot of the bed. 'She was often on that chair,' said Mary Ann, 'while Mrs Bravo slept. I said to her: "Will Mrs Bravo want anything else tonight?" She said: "That will be all. Take the dogs with you."' Mary Ann coaxed the two small terriers out of the bedroom and along the landing.

She was halfway down the stairs, the dogs following her, when the door of the spare bedroom was suddenly flung open. Mary Ann looked up in time to see Charles Bravo dash onto the landing, wearing his nightshirt, his face stricken with anxiety. He shouted: 'Florence! Florence! Hot water!'

Then he turned and disappeared back into his room.

CHAPTER SIX

'A Most Perplexing Illness . . .'

The single body on the drawing-room carpet is more
horrible and, indeed, more interesting than a dozen bullet-
ridden corpses down Raymond Chandler's mean city
streets. It is the contrast between order, normality, hierarchy
– and the dreadful and contaminating irruption of violent
death.

P. D. JAMES

Mary Ann stood where she was, frozen. She waited for Florence to
appear at the door of her bedroom, but no one in the house stirred.
There was a long silence. Slowly, the maid went back up the stairs
and knocked loudly on Florence's door. She entered the dimly lit
bedroom and found it exactly as she had left it a few moments earlier.
There was a fire burning in the grate but no other lighting. Mrs
Bravo was asleep in the big double bed, breathing heavily. The air
was lightly perfumed with the scent of alcohol. Beside the bed, still
fully dressed, sat Mrs Cox. She was knitting.

'Yes? What is it?' the housekeeper asked.

'You had better come quick. Mr Bravo is ill.'

Mrs Cox put her knitting onto the floor and silently crossed the
room, closing the door behind her. She swept across the landing to
the spare bedroom and disappeared inside. Mary Ann followed her,
lingering in the doorway.

The spare bedroom was also in virtual darkness. Here again, a fire
was burning in the grate, and the bedsheets were ruffled, indicating
that Mr Bravo had packed up for the night before being taken ill.

Now he stood at the window, which was open, vomiting onto the roof below. As Mrs Cox crossed the room towards him he turned around and again shouted for hot water. Then he fainted.

Bravo's collapse was sudden and spectacular. It had all the chief symptoms of a coronary. He turned slightly, seeming to spin on his heels, and slumped backwards as his knees gave way. Mrs Cox caught him, but she was a small woman, at least a foot smaller than he, and could do no more than break his fall as he hit the floor. At this point, Mary Ann crossed the room to offer help.

Mrs Cox felt for a pulse but couldn't detect one. She put her hand onto Bravo's chest and felt for the constant thump of his heart. She couldn't find that, either. She pulled open his nightshirt and began to massage his chest with her hands. 'Go downstairs and fetch some mustard and hot water,' she told the maid. 'Quickly.'

Mary Ann hurried downstairs. The house was in darkness now, most of the small gas lights having already been extinguished. She groped her way towards the kitchen, where a solitary light burned on the table. She found mustard powder in the cupboard, a bowl beneath the sink, and warm water in the kettle. She put the items on a tray and carried them back upstairs.

By now the panic was rising in her. When she got to the room she found that Bravo was still unconscious, and that Mrs Cox had taken to massaging his hands and feet, apparently to move his circulation. She put the tray down on the floor and tipped some of the hot powder into the bowl. But her hands were trembling. She was sure that Bravo was dead. She found herself unable to mix the solution, splashing small amounts onto the carpet. Eventually they poured a little of the solution down Bravo's throat and he immediately vomited. (Mrs Cox – according to her later evidence – was sure that she smelt chloroform in the vomit.) But when Mrs Cox tried to shake Bravo awake his head simply lolled back and forth in unconsciousness. She turned to the maid: 'Go downstairs and make some coffee,' she said. 'And tell the butler to send the coachman out to Streatham for Dr Harrison.'

Mary Ann got up again. She left the room and crossed the landing.

She passed Mrs Bravo's bedroom, where the door was still shut, and she froze. Charles Bravo was either dying or dead and no one had told his wife. She opened the door to the bedroom and went inside. Mrs Bravo was still asleep. She reached over and shook her awake.

'Umn . . . ?' murmured Florence.

'It's Mr Bravo,' said Mary Ann. 'You had better get up. He's very ill.'

The effect was startling. Florence pulled back the covers and leapt from the bed. She ran groggily across the landing to Bravo's room and burst inside. She took in the scene before her – her stricken husband, the little yellow pools of mustard, Mrs Cox's feverish attempts to revive him – and she became suddenly hysterical. What had happened? Was he breathing? What was the matter with him? Mrs Cox explained what she knew. He was still alive, she said, but only just. He was breathing but there was no pulse. He seemed to have swallowed chloroform. He had been sick a few moments ago and she could smell it on him. 'There's a bottle of it on the mantelpiece,' she said. 'But it's empty.'

Florence looked at the mantelpiece and saw a small glass bottle, with a tiny amount of green liquid in the bottom. She went over to Charles and knelt down beside him. 'Has the doctor been sent for?'

Mrs Cox nodded. 'I've sent for Dr Harrison.'

'*Harrison?*' bellowed Florence. 'He's too far! We need someone local!' She got up and ran for the door. 'Rowe! Rowe!' she screamed, running down the stairs.

The house was now on full alert. The butler had come out of his quarters on hearing Mary Ann running back and forth up the stairs and had gone down to the kitchen to question her. The cook was also coming down from the second floor. When Florence reached the bottom of the stairs she found the lights blazing and the front door ajar. 'Rowe?' she called. 'Rowe!' The butler emerged from the kitchen. 'Has Dr Harrison been sent for?'

'Yes,' came the reply. 'The groom has just left.'

'He'll take too long. Get someone local. Get anyone. I don't care who.'

Rowe went back into the kitchen and put on his coat. He would go out to the coachman's cottage and get him to ride into Balham to fetch Dr Moore. Dr Moore was only ten minutes away.

Florence returned to the spare bedroom, where Mary Ann and Mrs Cox were now trying to pour coffee down Bravo's throat.

'Dr Moore is coming,' said Florence, kneeling again beside her husband. She put her hand on his forehead. 'Try to wake up, Charlie,' she said. 'Please try.'

But Bravo slept on.

Dr George Harrison had been a practising physician for nineteen years. He had become Florence's local doctor after her move to the Priory, and had frequently attended her during her recent miscarriages. He had met her husband on only three occasions.

On the night of 18 April, Dr Harrison had been to a dinner in the City. He was already upstairs, about to undress, when he heard the sound of the carriage pulling into the driveway. There was a violent hammering at the front door. Dr Harrison went down to the hall. 'It was Mr Bravo's coachman,' he said, in court. 'He told me that Mr Bravo was ill and asked if I could come at once.' Picking up his Gladstone bag, Dr Harrison climbed into the carriage and set off for the Bravo house.

The journey from Streatham to Balham takes about fifteen minutes in a motor car. But in 1876 it was likely to take more than an hour, particularly if the weather was the bad, and it was dark. It was well past midnight by the time the carriage arrived.

On his arrival Dr Harrison was greeted at the front door by Mrs Cox. 'Thank goodness you came,' she said. 'Mr Bravo is very ill. I think he's swallowed chloroform. I smelt it on him when he was sick – and there is a bottle of it in his room which is empty.'

Dr Harrison said nothing. He climbed the stairs to the landing and crossed into the sickroom. In the doorway he was met by an old friend, Dr Joseph Moore, the local physician, who had arrived twenty minutes earlier. Dr Moore took him to one side. 'I told him that Mr Bravo looked as though he had been poisoned,' he said, 'though it was impossible to tell with which substance. I told him that Mr Bravo was, in my opinion, fatally ill. I also told him that I doubted whether he would live for more than about an hour.' He added that he had already injected brandy into the bloodstream in order to keep the heart going.

Dr Moore's diagnosis was a remarkable one. His arrival at the Priory had acted like a monastic command, and everyone had fallen suddenly silent. He had been told only that Bravo had collapsed and that various attempts to revive him had failed; no one had mentioned the fact that he had vomited; or that his nightshirt, which was soiled with vomit, had been swapped for a fresh one; or that the sick bowl into which he had been ill had been rinsed out. Nor had anyone mentioned that Bravo had been ill out of the window before collapsing, and that specimens of his vomit were lying on the leaded roof a few feet away. Furthermore, when Bravo had unconsciously passed a bloodied bowel motion in the bed, in the presence of Dr Moore, Mrs Cox had said: 'He's been drinking *red* burgundy all night.'

Dr Harrison followed Dr Moore back into the bedroom. He examined Bravo. He found that his pupils were dilated, his skin was cold and clammy, and his pulse, though weak, was racing. 'The aspect of the patient was like one in a state of drowsiness, following an epileptic fit,' he said. Dr Harrison knew at once what was wrong, and that Dr Moore had been right in his prognosis. He would give Mr Bravo an hour, but not much more. After examining him, Dr Harrison turned to the three women in the room and asked if they could account for his symptoms. But none of them seemed able to. Mrs Cox said that she had heard Bravo calling out and that he had collapsed as soon as she had reached him. Florence said: 'I think he must have had a heart attack. He went for a ride on a horse this afternoon, which bolted with him.' Then she had added that her husband was 'prone to fainting fits', and that he had been 'worried about stocks and shares'. Mary Ann said nothing.

'Well, it certainly isn't a fainting fit,' Dr Harrison replied. Then he said: 'I'm afraid that Mr Bravo is gravely ill. I am afraid he is unlikely to live.' Later he added: 'I told them both that he was dying. I told Mrs Cox that she was wrong – he hadn't swallowed chloroform, nor had he had a heart attack. I said that the symptoms were those of an irritant poison, such as arsenic. Mrs Bravo said: "Arsenic?" I said: "Yes." I asked if there were any poisons in the house. She replied: "Only rat poison, in the stables." When I asked if she could think of any reason why her husband would have poisoned himself she broke down. She told me that he had no reason to take any poison.'

The two doctors decided to mount a search of the bedroom, in an effort to trace the substance which Bravo had swallowed. The room contained a cupboard, stocked with clothes; a small wooden table, with a wash bowl and a lamp on it; and a bedside table, upon which a bottle and tumbler had been placed. On the mantelpiece, over the fireplace, there was a selection of harmless patent preparations and bottles of laudanum and chloroform, regular Victorian sleeping agents. There was also a large fire burning in the grate, but no evidence of anything having been thrown onto the coals.

With their search over, and no clue as to what he had swallowed, both doctors agreed that further help had to be sent for. Florence asked if she could summon Bravo's cousin, Royes Bell, a Harley Street surgeon, and his senior partner, Dr George Johnson, the Vice-President of the Royal College of Physicians. 'Mr Bell knows my husband's constitution,' she said. 'It is what they would both want.'

The two doctors immediately agreed. The carriage was despatched again, and the party waited, impotent.

Time must have ticked slowly in that dim little room: Bravo lying prostrate in bed, his breathing ragged, his pulse barely perceptible, apparently clinging to life by a thread; Florence lying beside him, slipping in and out of sleep; Mrs Cox carrying jugs of water, mixing mustard solutions, making coffee, bringing the doctors glasses of wine. Below, meanwhile, the servants gathered in the kitchen, anxious for news of their master, their livelihood.

'At every minute I was fearful that the heart's action would cease,' said Dr Moore, later. At last, there was the clatter of the horse and carriage coming up the Bedford Hill Road, and thundering into the long gravel drive of the house. Then there were voices in the hall, soft tread on the stairs.

Royes Bell was a general surgeon with a practice in Harley Street. Good-looking and cultured, Bell was already on the board of governors at King's College Hospital. At thirty-two, he was just over a year older than his cousin. 'We were like brothers,' he later told the Coroner's inquest. 'We were best friends. I liked and respected him immensely.'

Bell's colleague, Dr George Johnson, meanwhile, was one of the most famous physicians in London, a former President of the Royal College of Surgeons. It was agreed that Johnson would take charge of the case.

Within a quarter of an hour of their arrival, Charles Bravo suddenly began to show signs of returning consciousness. It took ten minutes for him to swim up to the surface. Then, at 2.45 a.m., he opened his eyes.

Bravo's first reaction on waking was to leap out of bed, apparently stricken by panic. He seemed to be trying to get out of the room. Eventually, with the combined efforts of the butler and two of the doctors, he was pinned back onto the bed, and Dr Moore administered a morphia suppository. 'Then the patient visibly calmed,' he said.

For a moment, Bravo seemed unable to comprehend either his surroundings or the identity of the people around him. He looked up at the collection of faces gathered around his bed, an audience waiting for an explanation, and sank back onto the pillow. The butler, Frederick Rowe, who was helping to change his sheets, remembered that he muttered: 'No laudanum, no laudanum . . .' as he came to. 'He did not seem to know either myself or Mrs Bravo,' said Mrs Cox, later. Florence, lying beside him, said: 'Charlie? Charlie?' But she got no response.

After a while, Royes Bell said: 'Charles? Do you know who I am?'

Bravo replied: 'Yes. You are Royes.' His voice was weak and hoarse.

'You have swallowed something,' Bell said. 'What have you taken?'

Bravo seemed confused. 'When he spoke his voice was feeble,' observed Dr Johnson, 'although his intellect seemed clear.'

Eventually Bravo replied: 'I rubbed my gums last night. For toothache. I used laudanum. I may have swallowed some.'

Dr Johnson interrupted: 'Laudanum will not explain your symptoms. You must have taken something else.'

Bravo thought for a long time. Then suddenly he shook his head. They began to think that he had not heard, or understood. 'No. I only swallowed laudanum. If it isn't laudanum, then I don't know what it is.'

Later, Dr Johnson would explain: 'Laudanum is a narcotic, generally taken for neuralgia. Mr Bravo said he had taken it for toothache and that is a common use. But it would not have caused his symptoms, even if he had swallowed a very large dose. Mr Bravo was clearly suffering from an *irritant* poison.'

Dr Johnson told Bravo that he was seriously ill. His digestive system was inflamed. There was a strong possibility that he would die. Then he told him that he had a moral obligation to confess to them if he had poisoned himself: 'If you die without telling us more than we already know,' he said, 'then someone will be accused of your death.'

Bravo nodded. 'I am aware of that. But I've told you all I can. I swallowed only laudanum.'

The little group of doctors moved away from the bed. The moment had passed. They were no further forward. Dr Johnson decided to start an anti-inflammatory treatment, if only to relieve Bravo's suffering. 'We will do what we can for you,' he said.

Later he stated: 'We agreed to give him cold milk and iced champagne as frequently as it could be taken, to foment the abdomen and to relieve the inflammation. We also agreed to give half a grain of morphia, as a suppository, as often as it might be necessary, to subdue the pain. There was nothing more we could do.'

As the doctors discussed how to proceed, Mrs Cox suddenly appeared at the elbow of Royes Bell. 'I wish to speak to you outside,' she said.

Leaving the sickroom, the two of them stepped out onto the landing. 'I must tell you that Mr Bravo *has* poisoned himself,' said the housekeeper. 'He told me that he had taken poison when I went into the room, just before he collapsed. He said to me: "I have taken poison – don't tell Florence." Then he fainted.'

Royes Bell could barely conceal his anger. 'Why haven't you told anyone this before now?' he thundered. 'It's no good sending for doctors if you don't tell them what's wrong.'

Mrs Cox replied: 'I have. I told Dr Harrison when he arrived.'

Royes Bell put his head around the sickroom door and called for Dr Harrison, who stepped out onto the landing, accompanied by Dr Johnson. At Bell's command, Mrs Cox then repeated her statement. Immediately Dr Harrison denied it. 'She did *not* tell me that Mr Bravo had poisoned himself,' he said later, at the inquest. 'She told me only that she thought he had swallowed some chloroform.'

It should be noted that chloroform was not regarded as a poison in the nineteenth century – it was a common painkiller, available without prescription, which could be found in most households. A modern comparison of this dispute might be between 'poison' and 'aspirin'.

As soon as Mrs Cox had made her statement, Dr Johnson returned to the sickroom and confronted Bravo. 'Mrs Cox tells us that you have confessed to taking poison,' he said. 'What is the meaning of this?'

'Did I?' replied Bravo. 'I don't remember . . .'

'You do not remember telling her that you had taken poison . . . ?'

Bravo shook his head. 'No, I don't remember at all. I only remember taking laudanum. I rubbed it on my gums.'

Dr Johnson and Royes Bell discussed bringing Mrs Cox into the sickroom, so that the dispute could be resolved. But they decided against any kind of confrontation that might antagonize the patient. 'Mr Bravo had made his denial,' said Dr Johnson, 'and he was so weak we thought it would be improper to challenge him.'

Royes Bell was suspicious now. He had known Charles since the age of five. They were best friends. As children they had played together on the beaches of Jamaica, camped out in the woods around St Ann's Bay. 'I knew that Charlie was the last person in the world to do something like this,' Bell said, later. 'He told me emphatically that he had swallowed only laudanum and I believed him.'

Bell decided to send a telegram to the Surrey Coroner's office and to the Detective Department at Scotland Yard. In the meantime, he also began his own inquiries at the Priory. His first task was to obtain samples of the food and wine that had been consumed at dinner. Rowe led the way across the hall and down a flight of dimly lit stairs to the pantry, where the cook, Ellen Stone, was making an early breakfast. Rowe told Royes Bell – insisted – that Mrs Cox and Mrs Bravo had eaten the same meal as the poisoned man. But he agreed that Mr Bravo alone had consumed burgundy. Bell took samples from the larder and the wine cellar, including five bottles of claret.

Upstairs, Bell searched the bedrooms. He removed the laudanum and chloroform bottles from the mantelpiece and emptied the drawers of the clothes chest. Then he went across the landing and searched Florence's bedroom, where he found endless homeopathic medicines – bottles of rosewater and tea-tree oil and peppermint fluid. He scooped everything into a box and had it placed in his carriage. Finally he went up to Mrs Cox's room, on the second floor. The housekeeper was asleep at that point, curled up for an hour in Florence's bed.

Mrs Cox's living quarters were characteristically impeccable: clothes neatly folded away, linen pressed. There were photographs on the bedside table of her three children and her sister. In the drawers of a small wooden chest there were personal letters, letters of reference, paperwork relating to her property in Lancaster Road. There was also a small bookshelf over the bed, on which Mrs Cox had placed more bottles of homeopathic remedies.

Outside, Bell searched the stables and the greenhouses. He took away samples of rat poison, weedkiller, embrocations, worming tablets. Then he went back into the house and told the servants that he wanted to question them. One by one they queued up outside the library – first the butler, then Mary Ann; then the cook and the head groom, finally the gardeners and coachmen. Each of them told him the same story: that Mr Bravo had appeared his usual self the night before; that the marriage had seemed happy; that they had all enjoyed excellent relations with him and his wife; that relations between Bravo and Mrs Cox had been cordial; that none of them could think of any reason why he would wish to commit suicide, nor why anyone would want him dead. 'I was not satisfied then and I am not satisfied now,' Bell said, later. 'Someone in the house knew the truth.'

But already Bell had an uneasy feeling. He knew that murder cases which involved poison always presented a classic problem: an opportunistic premeditation. The murderer operated in secret, planning their every move, striking at a moment when it was least expected, and then vanishing back into the normal fabric of the house. It was not like dealing with a shooting or a stabbing, often carried out in the heat of the moment, scattering clues for outsiders to retrieve. Whenever poison was used the murderer needed no alibi, and left no footprints.

Joseph Bravo had been at his holiday home in Sussex when the telegram had arrived from Florence. It read: 'Charlie is dangerously ill. Internal inflammation. Please come at once.'

'We set off immediately,' recalled Joseph. 'We arrived at the Priory just after lunch on the Thursday afternoon.' To everyone's surprise Bravo had made it through two nights, and was still clinging to his life.

On their arrival, the Bravos were met by Dr Johnson, who had told them that Charles had apparently confessed to taking poison. Joseph's reaction to that was 'Rubbish.' When Dr Harrison said to him: 'I may as well tell you — Mrs Cox has stated that your son has poisoned himself,' Joseph replied: 'I don't believe a word of it. It's nonsense.'

'I disputed it with Mrs Cox then,' he said, 'and I have disputed it throughout.'

Joseph Bravo's confidence stemmed largely from his reading of the young man's character. 'I brought him up from a child and I educated him,' he said. 'He was a man of great intellectual attainments. He was an Oxford man. He took an interest in all things and we debated everything. He was very level-headed and composed. He was always a man of the highest spirits. He was a very courageous man. He always held the theory that a man who took his own life was a coward. I spoke to him that morning, as he lay dying, and I asked him if he had poisoned himself. He told me most emphatically that he had not.'

After seeing his stepson, Joseph had a short interview with Florence, asking if she knew what had caused her husband's illness. She said she did not. 'Mrs Bravo never told me anything to account for his condition,' he recalled. 'She did not seem much grieved by it. The doctors had told her that his illness was mortal, but she did not seem much grieved in any way.'

Later, Joseph complained that Florence had given a catalogue of inconsistent explanations to account for her husband's illness. She had told Charles Bravo's former nanny that her husband had contracted food poisoning. But she had also spoken to Charles's cousin, and told her that his illness was simply a mystery that was unlikely ever to be solved. What Joseph did not yet know was that Florence had also volunteered other explanations, particularly to the physicians – claiming that Charles had been worried about stocks and shares, that he was prone to fainting, and that he had had a debilitating experience on his horse.

On Thursday, with her husband now slipping in and out of consciousness, Florence decided to make one last effort to save his life, and wrote to Sir William Gull, the most celebrated physician in England. Gull – Physician Extraordinary to Queen Victoria – had been knighted in 1871, after saving the life of the future King Edward VII, stricken with typhoid. He was 'the foremost opinion in London.' 'I believed that if anyone could save Charles,' Florence said, later, 'it was Sir William. I knew that he had saved people when others had given up all hope for them.'

Fortunately for Florence, Sir William was a close friend of her father, and frequently dined with him at the Reform Club. Mrs Cox had therefore been despatched across London, bearing the following note:

> Dear Sir,
>   My husband is dangerously ill. Could you come as soon as possible to see him? My father, Mr Campbell, of Buscot Park, will feel very grateful if you could come at once. I need not say how grateful I shall be.
>   Yours truly,
>   Florence Bravo

Gull arrived at the Priory at six-thirty that evening. A tall, imposing figure, he was known for his blunt and impatient manner, although he could be capable of acts of great kindness. After conferring with Dr Johnson, he went straight to Bravo's room and examined him. 'This is not disease,' he said. 'You are poisoned. Pray tell how it happened.'

Bravo replied, weakly: 'Laudanum. I took it myself.'

'You have taken a great deal more than laudanum, sir,' said Gull.

Then the familiar ritual of question and denial followed: 'You must tell us what you have taken. Or someone will be accused of poisoning you.'

'I am aware of that. But I cannot tell you anything more.'

'They tell me that you have eaten the same as everyone else. And I can assure you that laudanum will not have caused your illness. If you reveal the name of the poison, we could try an antidote on you.'

This was met with silence. Bravo 'closed his eyes and turned away'.

Sir William then left the room to confer again with Dr Johnson. Florence asked if there was anything that could be done to save her husband. Gull replied that he was sorry, there was not. 'I'm afraid that it wouldn't be right for me to give you any hope,' he said. 'The poison has penetrated into the tissues.' As Gull prepared to leave he was summoned back into the sickroom by Bravo.

The dying man was now an unnatural white. His breathing

came in thick, watery gasps. There was a perpetual layer of sweat across his face, which his mother fought repeatedly to remove with a cool sponge. 'The patient was then clearly in the last stages of his illness,' Sir William recalled, describing his 'pallid and sickly appearance.'

Bravo looked up as Gull entered the room and pulled the wet cloth off his forehead. 'I wish to tell you,' he said, 'that I have told you the truth and nothing but the truth. I have taken laudanum but I have not taken anything else.'

Gull felt 'very deeply moved' by the pitiful sight in the bed.

'I am afraid that laudanum will not account for your symptoms,' he said. 'You must think of the gravity of your situation. You must think of all you say and do.'

'I know that,' replied Bravo. 'But I cannot tell you anything more. I have told them all that I only took laudanum but none of them will believe me. I took it to rub on my lower jaw – like this . . .' He lifted his hand and feebly touched his mouth with his forefinger. 'Before God it was only laudanum,' he said. His voice cracked and he began to weep. 'If it wasn't laudanum, so help me God, then I don't know what it was.'

Six hours after Sir William Gull had left, around 3 a.m. on that Friday morning, Charles Bravo's system began to shut down. The pain had passed now, and he was in a state of enormous fatigue. He declined his wife's suggestion that they send for the rector of Streatham, but he did gather his family in the room to recite the Lord's Prayer. Then the group dispersed, leaving Bravo alone with his wife, mother and Royes Bell. It was apparent from his manner that he understood that he was dying. He had said to Sir William Gull, 'I know I am going to meet my Maker.' When Mary Ann Keeber entered the room to tidy up, he said: 'We shan't have our trip to Worthing now, Mary Ann; my next trip will be to Streatham Cemetery.' Later, he said to his wife: 'Make no fuss when you bury me.' He also made a will, in Florence's favour, which was witnessed by Royes Bell and by the butler.

At around 5 a.m., Bravo became unconscious. His pulse no longer responded to injections of brandy or to heart massage. He stopped breathing a few moments later, and was pronounced dead by Royes Bell at 5.20 a.m. on Friday morning.

It was fifty-five hours after his collapse.

CHAPTER SEVEN

The Investigation

'This is indeed a mystery,' I remarked. 'What do you imagine that it means?'

'I have no data yet. It is a capital mistake to theorise before one has data. Insensibly one begins to twist facts to suit theories, instead of theories to suit facts.'

SHERLOCK HOLMES AND DR WATSON,
Power and Influence

The police inquiries into Charles Bravo's death were hardly executed with military precision. Policing was slow to develop in Britain. Until the 1850s law enforcement relied on the traditional parish constable, an unpaid position, dependent on community support. And the empirical evidence suggests that men like Detective Chief Inspector George Clarke – assigned to the Bravo case – were unused to dealing with crimes involving murder. Ninety per cent of all crimes that the Metropolitan Police investigated in their first fifty years were crimes against property. It was therefore no wonder that solving a complex and mysterious poisoning case would prove to be beyond the capabilities of an average Victorian detective.

There were, naturally, other reasons for official hesitation. Chief Inspector Clarke and his men were not accustomed to the social milieu in which they found themselves. This, after all, was the upper classes. And they were not used to being questioned by policemen under suspicion of murder. Florence's father was a Justice of the Peace and a former High Sheriff. He owned land all over the world. He dismissed the police inquiries by saying that he could get a verdict of suicide 'in five minutes' if he wished. Later, he retained the services of Sir Henry James, one of Gladstone's closest friends. He also arranged for Queen Victoria's physician to give evidence on Florence's behalf. For Inspector Clarke and his men, it must have seemed as if they were chasing their suspects round some country house cocktail party.

The police inquiries did lead to a handful of important developments, however. The day after Bravo's death, Dr Joseph Payne, a pathologist from St Thomas's Hospital, performed a post-mortem, which revealed that Bravo had died after swallowing a massive dose of tartar emetic, a derivative of antimony. There were traces of it in his mouth, throat and stomach, where it had burned through the tissue lining his alimentary canal. But the worst damage was in the intestines, which had been blistered and swollen. The large intestine, in fact, had virtually disintegrated, eaten away by the corrosive poison.

Antimony, explained Dr Payne, was a highly caustic substance. It was a brittle, bluish-white metal. The oxide of the metal, when mixed with cream of tartar, produced tartar emetic, in the form of small white crystals. The crystals were lethal. In small quantities antimony had a diaphoretic effect, causing perspiration. In slightly larger doses it acted as an emetic, producing violent purging. The largest dose that a person could safely take – just three grains – would have a sedative effect, resulting in unconsciousness. A dose of four grains or more was usually fatal. Charles Bravo, said Dr Payne, had swallowed between thirty and forty grains, ten times the lethal dose. The poison had burned through the sensitive membranes of his digestive tract like fire through rubber. 'It must have been an agonizing death,' he said. The actual cause of death was heart failure.

The use of antimony had several implications for the police. Antimony was an unusual poison for a murderer to choose because it was very difficult to administer. It could not be tolerated in food or wine. Large amounts reacted with tannin and changed the colour of alcohol, making it cloudy and thickened. If it was mashed into someone's food they would be certain to vomit within a few minutes of eating it. If Bravo's dinner had been poisoned, or the burgundy at the table, then he would have been sick after only a few mouthfuls. 'I am certain that Mr Bravo was not poisoned during the evening meal,' said the pathologist.

How, then, might a poisoner have murdered him? Dr Payne had an answer: if the poisoner could have mixed the crystals of antimony with *water*, then they would have succeeded in killing Charles Bravo, because water was the one substance in which antimony was both soluble and tasteless. 'It dissolves best in hot water,' he said, later. 'But it will still dissolve in cold water pretty quickly. It will leave no taste. The person does not even realize they have consumed it.'

Had Bravo drunk a glass of water before going to bed? The butler did not recall him asking for water. But the maid Mary Ann Keeber did; in fact she had a vital statement to make on this question: 'I had the arrangements of the bedroom,' she told the police. 'I was instructed by Mr Bravo to fill a water jug each day for him. He would always drink from it last thing at night, before going to bed. He drank from it on the night he was poisoned because I remember filling it up the following day, while he was ill.'

Two days after Mary Ann had made her statement the police spoke to a friend of Bravo's who had shared rooms with him at Oxford. He also confirmed that Bravo had a habit of drinking water at bedtime.

Jephson Atkinson, who had known Bravo for twelve years, said he had 'observed' him doing this 'on numerous occasions.' 'It was an iron routine,' he added. Atkinson told the police: 'He used to drink from the water-bottle in his room or my room, or wherever he was, without using a tumbler. I visited his father's house about two years ago and saw he still had the same habit then, and I also observed it when we went to Paris together last year.'

The police were now certain that Bravo's water jug had been the agent of transmission. Someone had crept into the bedroom, tipped a sachet of crystals into the water, swirled it around, and then vanished. The unsuspecting man had then retired to his room and drunk from the poisoned jug. Within a few moments he would have begun to feel ill, as the poison seared its way through the lining of his gut. That was the moment when Bravo had raised the alarm.

Yet there were still those who were sceptical. How safe was it for the police to conclude that a crime had actually been committed, they argued. Wasn't it just as likely that Bravo had poured his own antimony into the water jug and had *intended* to kill himself, had been compelled by some strange motive which the police simply couldn't find? Two days after Clarke's conversation with Mary Ann, Sir William Gull broke his public silence on the case to voice his view that Bravo had killed himself. 'I saw not the slightest indication in his manner that he ever suspected anyone of poisoning him,' he wrote. 'He did not behave like a man who thought he was being murdered.' Gull believed that Bravo had gone to his room and deliberately swallowed antimony. Then he had lost his nerve. He had called for hot water as a remedy, to flush the poison from his stomach. He had told Mrs Cox what he had done. But he had refused to tell anyone else in the hope that he might recover. 'I can only speak of what I saw,' said Sir William. 'Mr Bravo was indifferent to his plight. If I were to tell a man that he was dying of poison and he showed no surprise, then that would lead me to think that he knew it already.' Sir William Gull was the most senior physician in England. He had been knighted by the Queen after saving the life of her son, stricken with typhoid, and his words carried enormous weight.

The next task for the police was to trace the poison. They organized searches of the registers of chemists in Surrey and south London – even in Worthing, where Mrs Cox had been on the day of Bravo's seizure. In the event it turned out that the antimony had been bought close to home; a chemist in Streatham had sold a large quantity of tartar emetic to a local man last summer.

The customer was George Griffiths, coachman at the Priory.

Griffiths had left the Bravo household in January and had taken up residence in Herne Bay, where he was employed by Lady Prescott. Griffiths confirmed to the police that he had used antimony in the treatment of horses throughout his employment with Mrs Bravo. He had learned about it as a young apprentice, from a manual called *The*

Farrier's Handbook. It was a highly effective way of worming them. Griffiths also said that he had kept the antimony in the stables of the Priory. It was usually made up into a liquid solution, he said, in a bottle marked *Poison*. But he had also kept it in its original crystal form, in packets. The antimony had been stored in a cupboard in the stables. As far as he knew, Mr Bravo had never removed any of the poison. But he could not be certain. Bravo often toured the paddocks, speaking to the staff. (In one of his letters he had said: 'I frequently go to the stables, over which I enjoy superintendence.')

'The cupboards were usually unlocked,' Griffiths added, 'and I was sometimes away from the Priory.' Asked if Mrs Cox or Mrs Bravo had ever requested antimony from him, Griffiths replied that they had not. Mrs Cox never spoke to him. Mrs Bravo often did, and was often alone in the stables. She also took a great interest in the welfare of the horses, he added, and was keen to know how they were being treated.

The statement by George Griffiths effectively marked the end of the police inquiry. Establishing the cause of death and tracing the poison was the easy part. Actually identifying the murderer, and building a convincing case against them, was to prove impossible. As Clarke knew, almost anyone in that household could have gone rummaging around in the stables for a toxic poison. A short acquaintance with a standard pharmacology textbook would confirm the mortal properties of antimony. But who amongst the eleven people that lived and worked in the building would have had a motive for murder? Who would have known of Bravo's habit of drinking water each night? And who would have had the opportunity to leave the poison for him?

Bravo's death had assumed a sort of Chinese intricacy, and these were questions to which the police would never be able to produce a plausible answer.

Chief Inspector Clarke's interviews with the occupants of the Priory were never less than clinical. But towards the end a perfunctory note seemed to creep into the proceedings.

Clarke interviewed Florence at her father's house in Brighton, and she met his questions with a cool equanimity. 'Except from what I know through Mrs Cox,' she said, 'I do not know how my husband came by his death. I am aware that he died from the administration of tartar emetic. But I do not know how he came by it.' Later she added: 'I have never purchased antimony in my life. I've never had it, and never heard of it as tartar emetic.' She dismissed the idea that she had a motive for murder – they had only been married five months and they had been trying to start a family. Clarke found Florence curiously detached during their interview, and concluded that she was on the edge of a breakdown. But he attributed this to the enormous pressure weighing on her from the recent newspaper publicity. 'She is reported to have brain fever,' he wrote.

Mrs Cox, on the other hand, gave a remarkably cool performance. She walked into the morning room at the Priory with a sense of resolve. Her eyes met the Inspector's, he recalled, and held them. She looked the picture of English respectability, in spite of her declining fortunes, and she remained confident and inscrutable throughout their interview.

Mrs Cox said that she had tried as hard as she could to save Charles Bravo on the night he was taken ill. 'All the doctors praised me for what I had done,' she said. 'No one said anything against me. His mother said to me: "You couldn't have done more to help Charles if he had been your own son."' She repeated her claim that Bravo had confessed to poisoning himself. 'He said to me: "I have taken poison, don't tell Florence,"' she recalled. She also denied knowing anything about antimony, or knowing that Bravo drank routinely from a water jug before going to bed. 'I never went near the stables,' she said. 'I had nothing to do with the horses. I wouldn't know antimony if I saw it. As for the water jug, I had no idea that Mr Bravo had such a habit. There was nothing in my duties which would take me into his bedroom at night, so I would not know of it.'

Clarke remained suspicious of the two women. But he knew that a criminal charge was out of the question. Even if one could establish a motive for Mrs Bravo, there was little incriminating evidence against her. She had not prepared her husband's food for him. Nor had she administered medicine to him during an illness. Her signature did not appear in any poison register as the purchaser of the chemical that had killed him. It was therefore impossible to charge her.

Mrs Cox was also insulated by the lack of direct evidence against her. 'There is strong feeling against Mrs Cox,' Clarke noted. 'The doctors in the case feel that Mr Bravo might well have survived if she had acted differently.' But being poor, and about to lose one's job, was not a motive that would stand up in court. It was true that she had had the opportunity to commit the crime. She had gone up to her room after returning from Worthing and had been alone there for several minutes. She could easily have slipped into the spare bedroom and poured a sachet of tartar emetic in Bravo's water jug. But no one had *seen* her doing this – no housemaid had watched her casually closing the door of his room as she returned downstairs – and without such testimony no indictment would succeed.

Clarke also interviewed James Gully in the last days of his inquiry. The two men talked for several hours and, like many of those who came within his aura, Clarke found himself increasingly spellbound by the charismatic doctor. 'He has a remarkable manner,' he noted, later.

Gully admitted that he had been Mrs Bravo's lover before her marriage and that this was something he deeply regretted. 'I feel my position most bitterly,' he said. He had received 'many threatening and abusive letters'. He knew that the story would break eventually and that he would be ruined. For the moment, it was only in Balham that people stared and spat at him as he walked the streets.

When Gully was asked about his feelings towards Charles Bravo, he replied: 'I was indifferent to him. I did not think of him at all.' The only time he had set eyes on Mr Bravo, he said, was when his carriage had drawn level with Mrs Bravo's in the street, and he had glanced out of the window. A young man inside was reading the newspaper. Then the carriages had driven on and the moment had passed. 'I looked inside because I was interested to see whom my young friend had married,' he remarked.

Almost ten weeks after Bravo's death, Clarke received a note from Superintendent Williamson. There had been a murder in Charing Cross, a woman's body had been fished out of the river. Would he log his files on Charles Bravo in the drawers of the Detective Department?

'During my long inquiry,' he wrote later, 'nothing was elicited to show how Mr Bravo met with his death.' Asked to give his private views on the case, he remained ambivalent. 'Mr Bravo must have taken the poison after entering his room,' he said, 'but whether it was with his own knowledge, or whether it was placed there secretly, I refrain from giving an opinion.'

Most officers who are forced to abandon an unsolved crime retain a degree of interest in it. They follow developments. They shadow the lives of the participants, hoping for some slip that might give them the opportunity to reopen their inquiry. Other officers send them wires. Journalists come and interview them. They live with the case, walk around it, dream of it, gossip about it. But none of this was for George Clarke. For Clarke, it was over.

Yet the story was not quite complete. There was still some kind of reckoning to come. Three months after Charles Bravo had been fatally stricken by poison, a Coroner's inquest was held in Balham, at the Bedford Hotel, attended by the nation's press. Hundreds of people lined the streets of the little village each day, hoping to catch a glimpse of the famous characters they had been reading about in their newspapers. At one point, when the proceedings coincided with a bank holiday, the Coroner was forced to suspend the inquiry, because 'half of London had converged on the pavements outside the Hotel.'

For Florence Bravo, the Coroner's inquest was the worst experience of her life. It had been called to consider the circumstances of her husband's death – indeed, the Attorney General himself had been instructed by the Home Secretary to represent the

Crown – and to determine whether anyone should be charged with his murder. But the court became increasingly preoccupied with the issue of Florence's relationship with James Gully, and each of the leading protagonists in the case was forced to disclose in lurid detail the history of the affair. This was the moment Florence had dreaded; the moment when her private 'lapses', as she called them, exploded onto the front pages of the newspapers. It was an indignity, a humiliation, that she found hard to bear. 'I shall not long survive this ordeal,' she said, at one point. 'Florence was utterly ruined by the inquest,' a member of her family told me. 'She was crushed by the revelations that came out about her private life.'

When the time came for her to give evidence, Florence tottered into the courtroom, holding onto the arm of her brother, the crowds crushing together to allow her through. *The Times* recorded that she wore a black dress and a widow's veil. She looked calm, according to one reporter, but it was not an indifferent calm. 'It was as if she was frozen,' he said. Three times during her testimony she broke down. She was pressed again and again in the hushed courtroom to admit details of her 'sexual conduct' with the elderly doctor: when had the affair started? How had it started? How long did her 'infatuation' last? When did she become pregnant? On and on it went, her replies telegraphed around the world by stringers from Australia, Europe and the United States. At one point she demanded that the Coroner protect her from the impertinent questions being asked by Joseph Bravo's solicitor. 'I refuse to answer any more questions about Dr Gully,' she shouted. 'This inquiry is about the death of my husband, and I appeal to the jury – as men and as Britons – to protect me.'

Gully, too, found the questioning 'a gross impertinence'. But his rebukes were more measured. 'I don't see the relevance of these questions,' he said.

'You are a witness here,' replied the Coroner, 'and not a judge of the relevance of questions.'

The circumstances of those extraordinary four weeks are documented in the verbatim transcripts of the Surrey Coroner's Office, and the daily bulletins of *The Times* newspaper, records of compelling interest. The narrative is that of a morality play, with its themes of erotic indulgence and recrimination; or perhaps a comic opera, with the elderly lover stumbling amongst his accusers. The script is written in dry, courtroom despatches: housemaids and stable boys recite their lines between the monologues of landowners, lawyers and politicians – each levelled to equality, just for a moment, by the due process of the law.

The drama chronicles one of the great social scandals of the nineteenth century, with all its ruinous confessions and revelations. 'This inquiry is the most disgusting exhibition to have been witnessed in this generation,' wrote *The Times*.

Yet for all its high drama the inquest produced nothing new in evidential terms, and the jury's verdict, when it came, was the only one that any sensible observers could have delivered:

> We find that Charles Delauney Turner Bravo did not commit suicide; that he did not meet his death by misadventure; that he was wilfully murdered by the administration of tartar emetic.
> But there is not sufficient evidence to fix the guilt upon any person or persons.

Two days after the inquiry ended the chief witnesses went their separate ways. Florence, shattered by the publicity, returned to Balham to oversee the sale of the Priory. She gave the servants their notice and said goodbye to Mrs Cox. Her father, it seemed, thought that the two women should be apart. Mrs Cox went north to Birmingham, moving into a house in Handsworth with her sister, in an attempt to find anonymity. She had received death-threats during the police investigation. Dr Gully, it was announced, was going to Austria.

Three weeks later Charles Bravo's mother supervised the building of a large stone surround over his grave at West Norwood Cemetery. It was her final gesture. Within a year she was also dead, apparently of haematemesis. Her husband told the press that she had succumbed to an 'inconsolable grief' after the mysterious death of her only son.

During the years that followed, while the protagonists remained alive, newspapers were constrained by the laws of libel from publishing the numerous theories that surrounded Bravo's death. By the turn of the century, however, when the case was already twenty-five years old, opinions were liberated, and books and newspaper articles began to appear. Mrs Cox had killed Bravo because she feared being dismissed, and had three children to support. 'After Mr Bravo joined the house the writing was on the wall,' said an article in the *Daily News*. 'She had to act decisively if she were to rescue her situation.' Agatha Christie contributed to a long article on the case for the *Sunday Times*, and said that Dr Gully had murdered Bravo, out of revenge and despair. Others said that Florence had killed him because he had grown impossible to live with. 'It was the only way of cutting short the married life that had become so intolerable to her,' said John Williams, the historian. Or perhaps his death was an accident – or simply suicide; why else had he remained silent on his deathbed? 'He was the last person in the world to keep silent if he thought he was dying by another's hand,' wrote Yseult Bridges in her book, *How Charles Bravo Died*.

Yet in reality no new evidence was ever produced to support the arguments, and no conclusive solution was ever found. In time, the case passed into the pantheon of English crime, a riddle that drew the interest and speculation of every passing generation. But it was part of its mythology, its attraction, that the crime could never be solved. 'If the Bravo case *had* been solved,' wrote Jonathan Goodman, the novelist, 'it would have taken away from us one of the greatest mysteries in modern crime.' The case would always remain 'the prize puzzle of British jurisprudence,' according to the Scottish writer, William Roughead. Behind the speculation, one simple fact governed: Charles Bravo was dead. And the secrets of his death had perished with him.

II

Who Killed Charles Bravo?

Does it appeal to our vanity, the notion that logic or
intuition or knowledge of the human heart can jump to
the conclusion which has escaped the experts and baffled
the police? Or is it fear that injustice has been done and
the wrong person convicted? Or that a murderer may
still be at large? I believe those old teamsters, vanity and
curiosity, play the strongest part, and that we all feel we
can complete these jigsaws with human pieces.

CYRIL CONNOLLY, *Sunday Times*, 1971

CHAPTER EIGHT

Vanity and Curiosity

More enthralling than a newly discovered murder case is a
new angle on an old one.

EDGAR LUSTGARTEN

Towards the end of the 1990s I began research into the death of
Charles Bravo as part of a documentary study for British radio. This
followed an academic study which I had originally undertaken in the
Department of English and Related Literature, at the University of
York. It was the beginning of a quest that would endure for many
months, that would take me around the globe in the search for clues,
but which would finally unravel the secrets surrounding Charles
Bravo's sensational death.

There were two clear strands underpinning my interest. First, it
was a great cause célèbre, focusing on issues about the nature of
Victorian society which are still relevant today. High-profile scandals
are rich territory for the writer because they generate massive
coverage of the lives of those involved. No detail is too insignificant
to titillate the newspaper reader. And so, with one of the great
crimes of the nineteenth century, we had a vivid portrait of a stratum
of society in the declining years of its existence.

The centrepiece of the story, of course, was the inquest, with
all its high drama and its bouts of moralistic bloodletting. The
sexual digressions had generated a storm of the most heated
Victorian rhetoric, and newspaper coverage of the case had eclipsed
news of Disraeli's negotiations with Egypt, the Indian tour of the
Prince of Wales, even the resumption of conflict in the Balkans. At

the same time, thousands of penny newspapers were sold, and little colour booklets, brightly illustrated with 'scenes from the Drama.'

But there was also no mistaking the resonance of the case as a classic unsolved murder. It echoed John Buchan or Conan Doyle, with all its twists and turns. The crime novelist, Henry Keating, who presumably knew a good plot when he saw one, had called it 'the most mysterious poisoning case ever.'

An elemental murder case almost always fascinates us. But the unsolved murder has its own particular, technical fascinations. As far as I could see, the central problem lay in constructing a theory that could plausibly assimilate all the established facts: if Charles Bravo had deliberately swallowed poison, why had he denied it to his family and his closest friend? And if he had been poisoned by *someone else*, why hadn't he shown even a passing interest in uncovering the identity of the poisoner? Why had Mrs Cox told so many lies? Why had Florence given so many implausible explanations for her husband's illness?

In due course I persuaded our production team that this was the right project for our programme, and began my preliminary research. It was the beginning of a quest that would perplex, amuse and irritate me for many months. I started at the British Newspaper Library in Colindale, where there were volumes of *The Times* going back to 1795. I combed through the intensive reporting of the inquest, line by line, examining the puzzle of logistics and motives. I also visited the British Library, raking through the books and articles on the case published in the last hundred years. The volume of material was enormous, and a strong testament to the compelling attraction of the story. A steady stream of books had been published and the case had been novelized and filmed.

Early on in my research I decided to make an unscheduled visit to Balham. I had been reading at length about the case, soaking up detail, and I wanted to see the bricks and mortal world that these people had occupied; to feel the very fabric of the story. It was to be a compelling experience.

I took the train across south London, with the intention of getting some work done as it shook itself along the tracks. But I became aware of a curious thrill when we reached East Croydon. Here were all those familiar place names: West Norwood, Streatham Hill, Tooting Bec Common. It was like being a small boy again, returning to the seaside, beginning an annual holiday that promised all kinds of new excitements.

The train stopped at Balham and I climbed out. Here was the same platform, now grey with rain, where Mrs Cox had met Dr Gully on that spring morning as she waited for the London train. I walked down the steps and out into the street.

Of course it was different – cars and cabs and lorries; people bustling in and out of modern shops; all the famous names of the High Street. And yet it was not so different that Florence or Mrs Cox, standing beside me, would have failed to recognize it. The layout of the streets was the same; the frontages were still deter-minedly Victorian, with their dark stone and large bay windows. I turned left and began to walk up Bedford Hill Road.

After a few moments I came to the Bedford Hotel, the place where the inquest had been held, where George Griffiths had sat at the bar chatting to the manager that morning in December. I walked in and ordered some coffee.

Here it was as if nothing had altered: large open fires, curling brass chandeliers, thick velvet drapes. Even the wooden floors were the same. I fell into conversation with the manager, who smiled as soon as I mentioned why I was in Balham. 'It's mainly Americans we get,' he said. 'I think it's all a bit ghoulish.'

The Bravo case was still much talked of amongst local people, he said, particularly the older ones, who had lived in Balham all their lives. Everyone had their views on the case. People had been told stories by their mothers and grandmothers. When I had finished my coffee I asked him to show me the room upstairs where the inquest had been held. He fetched a set of keys and we disappeared through an oak door.

We climbed the steps up to a large landing. It was eerily silent.

Our feet clumped on heavy oak. 'There were so many people here they had to get a surveyor in,' said the manager. 'They didn't think the floors would stand the weight.' He unlocked the door and pushed it open.

For a second I felt I was back in 1876. The manager of the pub was out on the landing, trying to find the lights, and I was alone in the room. The only illumination came from the street lights outside, penetrating the long arched windows, giving a silvery glow to the atmosphere. I had seen a contemporary illustration of the courtroom and found it now to be almost exactly as it had been at the time of the inquiry – the panelled walls, the creaking, lacquered floor, the high ceiling. A dozen of the most distinguished lawyers in England had occupied this room for five tortuous weeks; the Attorney General, the Treasury Solicitor, even Gladstone's Home Secretary, Sir Henry James.

I left the Bedford and headed north towards the Priory. I knew that no one investigating the case had managed to obtain proper access to the house since the turn of the century. (Before the war it had been owned by a family who had resolutely refused to accommodate inquiries. In more recent years it had been split into flats, and the room where Bravo had died – the room I particularly wanted to find – was part of a one-bedroom apartment. A few years earlier an ITV producer had tried to obtain permission to visit, in order to authenticate his production. But the tenant had turned him away at the door: it was private property, he'd said.)

I passed Orwell Lodge, Dr Gully's house, and walked up the Bedford Hill Road towards Tooting Bec Common. How many times had Gully himself walked this route, on his way to make love to his mistress? How many times had Florence strolled down here? Or Bravo himself, hurrying to catch a train to take him to his chambers? The process of writing is a solitary one, and sometimes the characters seem to be nothing more than the occupants of your own private world. But Balham reminded me that these were real people and that they had lived ordinary lives. They were no longer a part of my world; I was suddenly in theirs.

'You'll know you're there,' the landlord had said, 'because the road ends and you're almost on the Common.'

The houses on either side abruptly vanished and I breathlessly turned left into the driveway. Through a clearing of oaks I saw flashes of white plaster, and then suddenly it was there, in front of me, dense and still.

It had a curiously artificial look to it, like a house out of fiction; like stumbling on Manderley or Netherfield. Furthermore, the ten acres of grounds and gardens, which Florence had so carefully tended, had been urbanized, and the house was hemmed in on all sides by red brick. The oak tree that Florence had planted in the front drive continued to flourish. But the railway line cut a straight path through the grounds to the west. The brick and metal landscape gave the house a disjunctured appearance, as though it had been wrenched from its natural surroundings and dropped, at random, into the modern world. But there was no denying its inherent beauty, its symmetry and neatness. It looked on that chilly winter evening much as it must have looked when Florence fell in love with it in the early spring of 1872.

I walked up to the porch. Two large glass doors revealed a dimly lit entrance hall. Dr Moore had stood here, waiting for Mrs Cox to let him in and take him up to the patient. Inspector Clarke had stood here, too, ready with his search warrant.

Inside, on the other side of the glass, the atmosphere looked thick and gravely subdued. There was little to suggest the twentieth century. Even the wall lights were Victorian.

There was an intercom on my left. I pressed it and waited. Eventually a young voice answered. I introduced myself, explained that I was a journalist interested in the Bravo story, and asked if it would be possible to see inside the building. After some reluctance the young man said that he would come down to the hall.

It was dark now. The wind had whipped up and was lashing rain against the side of the building. I gazed upwards and saw a light on in Florence's old bedroom, the curtains open, a picture hanging on the wall. Someone had hung a dress to dry on the curtain rail.

Finally, the tenant appeared. His eyes were suspicious. Why hadn't I telephoned or written? It wasn't convenient. His girlfriend was in the shower. They had both just finished work. They were tired. They were getting ready to go out. We talked a little more, about the house, about Bravo. And eventually, in an act of great kindness, he agreed to show me around.

I crossed the threshold into the warmth of the hall and he closed the door behind me. The atmosphere was startling. The walls were covered in chocolate-brown paper. There was a chocolate-brown carpet on the floor. I could see the doors of the study and the morning room, painted bright red and encased by white frames. In the right-hand corner there was an oil painting under a brass spotlight, and a polished oak table with fresh flowers on it. But there were no other furnishings. A sense of understated opulence was everywhere. It was dark, too, the only light coming from two brass wall fittings.

I had been expecting the inside of the Priory to disappoint me, to look so modern that it would be impossible to envisage the atmosphere in which Charles and his household had lived. But it didn't disappoint. There was no linoleum or bright plastic. There wasn't even a telephone. To my amazement it looked as it must have looked a century ago. I could easily see Mrs Cox gliding about the rooms, Florence sweeping down the stairs.

We crossed the hall, passed the dining room, and began to mount the staircase. The stairs were dark and wide. An oak banister twisted and curled in my hand. On the landing there was a portrait of Florence. 'There's the lady herself,' said the young man, casually.

We reached the top of the stairs. Here was the landing where Charles Bravo had stood on the night of his collapse, shouting for hot water. We entered Florence's old bedroom. It had been divided into three small rooms: a bedroom, kitchen and bathroom. At the window one could look out across the gloom to the fields of Streatham Common, where Florence had walked with Gully and raced her cobs. Bravo's bedroom was now a living room. The television set glowed from the corner. Although it was the room where Bravo's family had gathered as he lay dying, where Dr Johnson and Dr Moore had frantically searched the drawers for poison, it now seemed like any sitting room of the comfortable middle classes.

During my visit I checked measurements, memorized the layout of rooms, and generally acquainted myself with the exact geography of the place. This was more than merely a quaint obsessiveness, however; it was to be an important exercise in gathering evidence.

As I came to leave a sudden thought occurred to me. There was supposed to be a ghost. *Was* there a ghost? One of Robert Campbell's descendants had told me that the Priory was known to be haunted. She herself had spoken to a woman who had visited the house and slept in Bravo's old room. Shortly before dawn, the woman had said, the room had grown very cold. She had become aware of a presence near to her. She had turned over to find a man standing at the foot of the bed, staring at her. Eventually the apparition had vanished. Unable to sleep, she had woken her host, who had shown her a photograph of Charles Bravo, and she had confirmed it as the figure she had seen in the bedroom. Her host had not been surprised. People often complained of noises, of an atmosphere, of objects being moved. He had thoughtfully veiled this from her before putting her in the room.

Had this merely been an invention of the imagination, the mind playing tricks in that twilight world between sleeping and waking? I debated whether it would be fair to tell the young man about this, and had just decided against it, when he said: 'Of course we have a ghost. At least, we *had* a ghost.'

'Really?'

'Um. I never saw it. My girlfriend saw it a lot. She often sits up late. She would hear noises. She saw him once in the hall.'

I confessed to knowing a little about this, and told him the account that had been given to me. He listened intently. Then he sighed: 'Well, it's over now.'

'Is it?' I asked.

'Yeah, it got so bad that we decided to get a priest in to perform an exorcism. He came three weeks ago. We've had no trouble since then.'

The noise of the shower stopped abruptly. It closed the subject. The young man moved to leave the room. He led me back down the stairs, wishing me luck with my project, and we shook hands in the hall. Outside, I hurried back in the drizzle towards the railway station.

I had decided as soon as I started my research that a fresh approach was needed if the case were ever to be solved. None of the books, articles or television programmes had managed to produce a definitive solution, because they were sourced solely from the newspaper accounts of the inquest. The simple fact remained that no plausible answer to the mystery was possible on the existing evidence.

I therefore started by scrapping the secondary accounts of the story and returning to the original sources. With the help of a senior archivist at Scotland Yard, I unearthed the files of Detective Chief Inspector George Clarke, the statements of witnesses, the reports of scientific experts. I also studied the Home Office files. At the same time, I embarked on an operation to trace the descendants of those who had originally been involved. My fellow journalists thought this a pointless exercise; an example of growing monomania. But I felt that a search for descendants might itself throw light on the mystery, given the strong oral traditions that exist in families, and the propensity for secrets to pass from one generation to the next in diaries or letters. Unfortunately, one of the consequences of the lack of original research was that no one knew what had become of the central characters: how long they had lived, where and how they had died, and whether they had any descendants. Mrs Cox had last been heard of in Brighton at the turn of the century. Florence had left the Priory in 1877 and had gone to live a secluded life on the south coast. *The Dictionary of National Biography* records that James Gully had died, aged seventy-seven, in 1883. But that was the extent of the available information.

The first people I managed to trace were the Campbells. They were surprisingly difficult to find. Buscot had been sold long ago, and none of the usual biographical or business directories was of any use. It was as if they had vanished off the face of the earth. This was especially curious because of their formerly prominent social position. Later I learned that the disappearance of the Campbell family was a direct consequence of Charles Bravo's death. They had been utterly ruined by the scandal.

I finally traced the family after an amazing stroke of luck. In the early weeks of my research I visited the churches around Buscot, where members of the family are buried. At each church I made a point of looking through the visitors' book, in case any Campbell descendants had visited the graves of their ancestors. At Faringdon this search paid off. A descendant of Robert Campbell – his great-great-granddaughter – had left a New Zealand address. My contact with them then led to other family members – Robert Campbell had been a prominent politician on South Island, sitting in the State Legislature. So had William and Stuart Campbell, whose descendants were scattered across both Australia and New Zealand. I made immediate arrangements to travel to the Pacific Rim, to interview William's great-great-grandchildren, who had become custodians of the family records. During my visit, the Campbell family were to provide me with much new information on Florence, and on how the scandal had affected her. They were also to bring Florence and her parents to life, fleshing out bare historical details. It was the first source of 'inside' information that I obtained.

At the same time I also traced the Ricardo family, who were now living on the English south coast, Malta and Australia. To my surprise they were still in touch with the Campbells. 'We all had a very jocular chat about the case some time again,' said Lt. Col. Peter Ricardo, when I spoke to him. But my most rewarding moment came when I made a crucial discovery about Jane Cox, which was to change the whole complexion of the story. The Cox connection took me to Jamaica, to the archives of the National Library in Kingston and Spanish Town. It was here, amid papers and files dating back more than a century, that I finally unlocked the secrets of Charles Bravo's death.

There were areas where I suffered setbacks, however. And these often served to remind me that I was not dealing with a dry, historical inquiry, but with a family tragedy that had touched the lives of many people. My attempts to make contact with the Gully family, for instance, were less than successful, and provided clear evidence of the sensitivity that is sometimes aroused by journalists. Having traced James Gully's great-grandson, Viscount Selby, through modern editions of *Who's Who*, I wrote to him at the House of Lords, explaining that I was researching the life of his great-grandfather and asking if he could assist me. I wrote three times and telephoned twice. I failed to receive a single reply.

As the months rolled by, and my investigation took me from one side of the globe to the other, all kinds of sources came forward with information: academics, medical experts, local historians. But it was the search for descendants and the new material that they produced that provided the most rewarding aspect of the inquiry. It was proof that – even after 125 years – one could still go back and pick up the threads of the old investigation.

I decided to begin where Chief Inspector Clarke had left off; I felt the problem with his inquiry had been one of approach. Instead of narrowing his list of suspects he had actually enlarged it, and his inquiry had subsequently run out of steam. If one was going to discover the truth about what had happened to Charles Bravo, one had to begin with a process of elimination.

CHAPTER NINE

'The Curious Demeanour of the Dying Man'

The curious demeanour of the dying man – who was not indifferent to life, but utterly indifferent to the cause of his own death – unsuspecting, casual – was so strange it defies conjecture.

Daily News, 12 August 1876

The first possibility to consider was that Charles Bravo had indeed committed suicide. Suicide had been the verdict of several of those who had studied the case, including Sir William Gull, the Queen's Physician. Sir William believed that Bravo had retired to his room, swallowed antimony, lost his nerve and summoned help.

At least one book was published outlining this view.

Gull's theory had endured for over a century, and was rooted in one overriding observation: Charles Bravo's indifference as he lay on his deathbed. Bravo, he said, had been ill for over fifty hours. He had spoken to his friends and to his family. He had been told that the substance he had admitted taking – laudanum – would not account for his symptoms. He had been told that he was poisoned. And yet in spite of this, *he did not once accuse those around him of trying to kill him. He did not treat anyone with suspicion. Nor did he demand any kind of inquiry.* This was especially strange in the light of Charles Bravo's own circumspect character. None of us would be casual about the cause of our own impending death, Sir William argued, unless, of course, we were disturbed enough to be responsible for it. The only plausible deduction, then, was that Bravo *knew* what he had taken.

'It would be surprising to me if I were to tell a man that he was dying of poison and he was not surprised,' Sir William had said. 'It would lead me to think that he knew it already.'

The second reason for supposing suicide was Mrs Cox's statement. She said that Bravo had 'confessed' to her that he had swallowed poison as he stood vomiting from the window. Although her statement was met with some disbelief it was impossible for the police to rule it out completely. 'He said to me: "I have taken poison – don't tell Florence",' she claimed.

But *had* Bravo killed himself? Was Sir William Gull correct? Where was his motive? And how had he accomplished it?

Personally, I had very strong doubts that Bravo had taken his own life. Some of this was rooted in nothing more than an intuitive reasoning of the evidence about his life and character; some of it was more evidentially based. It was interesting to note that none of the six doctors involved in the case, except Sir William, believed that the man in front of them was dying by his own hand. Nor did any of the lawyers who were subsequently consulted.

The first problem in the suicide theory is the lack of motive. I had begun my investigations by consulting the files of Detective Chief Inspector George Clarke, who had extensively tracked Bravo's past in an effort to find evidence of financial or private problems. I also contacted the family of Bravo's partner, Edward Hope, to assess what I could of his professional life. Hope's granddaughter, Lady Nairne, was still alive and living on the south coast, surrounded by papers and documents relating to their practice in Essex Court.

The notes made by Chief Inspector Clarke gave a clue to the investigator's exasperation. 'I can find no motive whatever for Mr Bravo to have taken his own life,' he said. Clarke records a visit he made to The Temple, soon after Bravo's death, to inspect his desk and files. He had spent a whole afternoon going through the paperwork: files on past cases; details of the forthcoming Quarter Sessions in Brighton; reports from the southern circuit; copies of newspapers, and endless stacks of correspondence. The vast oak surface was crammed with literature. But none of it hinted at scandal or blackmail – there was no suggestion of financial or personal problems. Bravo's diary, he said, revealed only the routine engagements of a rising young barrister: professional lunches, dinners, social functions, appearances in court, meetings with clients. 'There is nothing to account for his being in a state of mind to commit suicide,' he concluded.

These words were borne out by the descendants of Bravo's friends, Frederick MacCalmont and Jephson Atkinson. The case had been much talked about within the families, and there was great scepticism that Bravo had killed himself. Whenever the subject was discussed, Edward Hope referred people to a dinner he had had with Bravo a few days before his death, where he had been struck by Bravo's ebullience and plans for the future. According to Hope, Bravo had talked of the forthcoming general election, where he had hopes of entering Parliament.

In addition to this, there were the objective accounts of Bravo's own behaviour in the period leading up to his illness. There had clearly been nothing in his manner suggesting that he would soon attempt suicide. He met people socially and made plans. He consumed three large meals on the fatal day, enjoyed a Turkish bath, took vigorous exercise. Two days earlier he had played tennis, badgered a friend to come and stay, walked about the garden quoting Shakespeare. None of this was consistent with the temperament of a man who was about to destroy himself.

There was also a further reason, I discovered, why Bravo's death did not make sense as a suicide: the use of antimony as the means of death. According to toxicologists, potassium antimony is one of the most corrosive substances known to man. When it is swallowed in large doses it will produce an excruciating reaction. 'Its caustic nature produces a terrible, lingering death,' said Dr Johnson, at the inquest. 'Antimony is a rapidly acting chemical which corrodes the mucous membranes,' said Dr Moore. 'Death is especially painful with antimony.' Bravo had indeed 'screamed with pain' as he lay dying. He had endured nearly three days 'of the most terrible agony'. In fact, his reaction to the poison was one of the most harrowing aspects of the entire case. How could he have chosen such a terrible end for himself?

Of course it could be claimed that Bravo did not *know* that potassium antimony had such a corrosive nature; that he may have imagined it would carry him off quite painlessly. But there is strong evidence against such an idea. First, Bravo's uncle Henry Smith, a surgeon at King's College Hospital, told *The Times* that Charles had 'a great interest' in medicine, drugs and surgery: 'He would often come to King's College Hospital to watch operations being performed,' he said. Second, I discovered while researching Bravo's career as an undergraduate at Oxford University that *he had studied medical jurisprudence as part of his degree*. According to the alumnus records of Trinity College, Bravo had studied the subject in 1866. The clinical and criminal use of antimony would certainly have been part of his syllabus.

From this evidence, then, it is reasonable to assume that Bravo would indeed have been familiar with tartar emetic, and would have known all about its corrosive characteristic. He would certainly have familiarized himself with it if he intended to use it as a means of committing suicide. And his acquaintance with the poison would surely have prevented him from using it as a means of killing himself. 'No one wishing to commit suicide,' said the pathologist, Dr Joseph Payne, 'would have done so with one of the most painful chemicals in the entire pharmacopoeia.' It is interesting to note that there is not a single case of suicide with antimony known in the western world.

Yet if Bravo's death was *not* suicide, as this evidence suggested, how did one explain Mrs Cox's claim that Bravo 'confessed' to her? And how could one resolve the argument made by Sir William Gull: the puzzle of Bravo's silence on his deathbed? Disproving Mrs Cox's story was easier than I had thought. Indeed, it was startling to think that the police had not used the same method that I employed, more than a century later, to discount her story.

Let us go back for a moment to the sequence of events outlined by Mrs Cox. She told the police that she entered Bravo's room, crossed to help him, heard his 'confession' of suicide and watched him collapse. It was a simple, straightforward account of events, apparently beyond contradiction. Yet I remembered from Mrs Cox's own evidence that there had actually been a third person with her in the bedroom when Charles collapsed. *This was the maid, Mary Ann Keeber.* When I looked over her testimony at the inquest, I was interested to discover that Mary Ann – who had been in the doorway when Bravo fainted – *had failed to hear him making any 'confession' to Mrs Cox*. Mary Ann agreed that Mrs Cox was next to Bravo as he stood at the window, and agreed that he shouted for hot water. But at no time, she said, *did he confess to taking poison*. He simply called out and then fell into unconsciousness. By Mary Ann's account, therefore, no 'confession' was ever uttered.

Of course, one possible explanation for this discrepancy between the two women is that Mary Ann simply did not *hear* the 'confession' made to Mrs Cox. Charles was standing at the window, after all, and Mary Ann was in the doorway. They were separated by a bed. If Charles had *whispered* to Mrs Cox, how likely was it that someone on the other side of the room would have heard him?

In an effort to resolve this question I performed an experiment at the Priory, in the room where Bravo was taken ill – just as the police should have done in 1876.

The window from which Bravo had vomited that night has now been bricked over, but in every other respect the room remains the same. By repeating Bravo's alleged 'confession' in a variety of pitches, I was able to establish that a person of *normal* hearing – standing where Mary Ann had stood in the doorway – *would certainly have heard* any remarks uttered in the dense stillness and silence of that small area. I was satisfied that the maid would have witnessed anything that Charles might have said.

Why, then, had Mrs Cox lied? Why had she fabricated a confession of suicide? The answer was simple: by the time she came to make her police statement she was conscious of the strong feeling against her. 'It is dreadful to have such things said as they are now saying,' she wrote. She needed to invent a story that would deflect suspicion. Mary Ann, she knew, was a junior member of the household, a mere girl, whose statement would be either overlooked or treated without merit. The fact that Mrs Cox fabricated a confession does not mean, of course, that she was the murderer; it merely means that she was anxious to avoid a capital charge.

Yet Mrs Cox's claim, and the whole theory of suicide, would never have endured had Charles Bravo not himself given the appearance of taking his own life by remaining so curiously silent on his deathbed. Here, after all, was the crux of the case: why had Bravo shown no interest in his condition, nor accused anyone of poisoning him, unless he was responsible for what had happened? 'My husband never showed any suspicion towards anyone of having poisoned him,' said Florence. 'I never once saw him concerned by what the doctors said,' recalled Robert Campbell. 'He was never suspicious of anyone else.' 'Only someone who had poisoned himself would have been so casual,' Sir William had told the Coroner.

Of course, there was a simple explanation: Bravo, having deliberately swallowed poison, hoped that he might recover. If he did so he would be prosecuted for attempted murder, since suicide was still a criminal offence. 'As a barrister,' said Dr Andrew Haynes, a senior lecturer in law, whom I interviewed at the beginning of my research, 'Mr Bravo would naturally have known that if he tried to kill himself and then made a recovery he would be charged with a serious crime. So he had a very strong motive for staying silent. He would also have known that a Victorian clerk – called John Parsons – had already survived being poisoned with huge doses of antimony by the murderer, William Palmer. Parsons' life had been saved by immediate vomiting. So the possibility that Bravo might recover remained a reasonable one, in spite of what the doctors told him. Furthermore, Charles Bravo would have also known that it would be impossible for the police to charge an innocent person with his murder provided he remained silent while he was ill. Ethically, this would have enabled him to resist all that pressure to confess.'

Yet we have already discounted both Bravo's motive for suicide and his alleged 'confession' – and we have shown that no one would

Florence and Alexander
soon after their wedding.
(*James Ruddick*)

Captain Alexander Ricardo,
Florence's first husband,
aged 22 years old.
(*James Ruddick*)

Charles Bravo, five months
before his death.
(*Hulton Getty*)

Dr Gully's clinic, the Hydro,
separated into male and
female quarters by the Bridge
of Sighs. The doctor's affair
with Florence began when
she was a patient here.
(*James Ruddick*)

Dr James Gully, Florence's lover, whose patients included Dickens, Disraeli, Gladstone and Charles Darwin. (*Hulton Getty*)

Jane Cox, 'a shrewd and remarkable woman', photographed just before the murder. (*Hulton Getty*)

Buscot Park, the Campbells' family home. (*The National Trust*)

The Priory, Balham. (*Bernard Taylor*)

A drawing from 1876 shows the layout of the landing at the Priory, with the bedrooms of Florence (C) and Charles (B). (*The British Library*)

A contemporary illustration of the room where Charles died. Note the proximity of the door to the window. (*The British Library*)

Mrs Cox giving evidence at the Coroner's inquest. (*Hulton Getty*)

The front page of *The Pictorial World*.
(*The British Library*)

The search for the poison.
In due course it was convincingly
traced back to the Priory.
(*Metropolitan Police*)

The author searches for Mrs Cox's descendants in the West Indies.

Content, Mrs Cox's vast plantation estate in Golden Valley, Jamaica, recently uncovered by the author.

THE JAMAICA ARCHIVES

SPANISH TOWN,

JAMAICA

Monumental Inscriptions of Jamaica:
Page 267 St. Ann

Henry Cox, of Content, in the parish of St. Ann, d. 3rd November 1855, aged 52.

Return of Properties
1882

Name of Property - Content
Extent - (acreage) - 690
Common Pasture and Pimento (acreage) - 313
Wood and Ruinate (acreaage) - 357
Name of Owner - John Leslie Cox
Person in occupation or charge - John Leslie Cox

Letters of Testamentary, 1B/11/18/55, Folio 136

On the 20th day of May 1879 the last Will and Testament of Margaret Cox was proved... and she did nominate Jane Cannon Cox to be the Executrix thereof....
Signed the 14th day of June, A.D. 1879

Goods of the house of Content, in the ownership of John Leslie Cox... as they were proved by Mrs Jane Cox the Executrix of the Will of Margaret Cox, we certify under our hands and seal this 13th day of August 1879

Barcley Chadwick

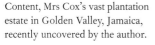

New evidence from the Jamaica Archives, showing the extent of Mrs Cox's fortune. (*James Ruddick*)

Florence on the eve of her wedding to Charles Bravo. (*Hulton Getty*)

choose to kill themselves using the chemical with which he was poisoned. So, was there another explanation for his strange behaviour on his deathbed? Was it possible that Bravo could have remained silent for some reason other than self-interest? Indeed, my researches revealed that there was: it could not have been uncovered by the police – nor articulated by the doctors at the time. But it was available to any modern investigator examining the properties of potassium antimony tartrate that have been established by modern science.

In the autumn of 2000 I contacted Dr John Vale, Director of the West Midlands Poisons Unit, one of the largest toxicology labs in Britain. I also consulted textbooks at the Wellcome Medical Library, spoke to staff at the National Poisons Unit in east London, and conducted an extensive interview with Dr Benjamin Jacoby, a Cambridge scientist specializing in biochemisty. I discovered that poisoning with antimony tartrate has a particularly unpleasant side-effect: it produces a strong, paralysing effect on the central nervous system. In high doses it will affect its victim's neurological responses, particularly in the twenty-four-hour period prior to death. *In fact the curious reactions exhibited by Charles Bravo as he lay dying are entirely consistent with the effects of antimony on the human brain.*

The definitive textbook on toxicology is *Martindales*, published annually for use by clinicians dealing with acute poisoning cases. *Martindales* confirms that patients suffering from acute antimony poisoning will experience 'profound dehydration, collapse, shock and death. Patients who survive the initial effects may develop severe peripheral neuropathies [defined as "confusion, anxiety, lassitude and depression"].'

Later, when I interviewed Dr Benjamin Jacoby, I learned more: 'Exceedingly high doses of antimony will certainly produce an effect on the central nervous system,' he said. 'Its pathology is similar to that of arsenic trioxide. Patients typically experience a severe sense of confusion and a general neuropathy. They might also be expected to exhibit symptoms of acute depression.' Dr Jacoby added: 'Every case will vary, but the behaviour of Charles Bravo after his seizure does not puzzle me at all: it is entirely consistent with the impact of a trivalent poison.'

Confusion and depression? These were the classic symptoms of Bravo's illness. When he first opened his eyes he didn't know where he was. He couldn't recognize anyone in the room. 'He did not know Mrs Bravo or myself,' reported Mrs Cox. Dr Harrison said: 'It was a long time before he was able to recognize his wife.' And Mary Ann said: 'I think he did not know me.' The only person he recognized was Royes Bell, whom he had known since the age of five. When Dr Moore came to leave the Priory, some twelve hours into Bravo's illness, the dying man shook him by the hand and told him that he looked forward to seeing him again when he had fully recovered. Clearly, Bravo was too confused to understand what had happened.

Later, however, as the system shook off its paralysis, his sense of confusion lessened. He started to recognize people. He talked coherently. He realized that laudanum didn't explain his illness. But by then a deep and profound depression had started to overtake him. He wept. He said prayers. He listened to what people told him but he didn't respond. The best he could do was ask feebly whether he would continue to suffer such terrible pain. 'Clinical depression would almost certainly be present in a very acute form if the patient lived long enough,' Dr Jacoby told me. 'The patient would be unable to organize a proper mental response to what he was told.'

It is interesting to note that the doctors in the case – while not understanding the precise mechanisms of his neurological response – were able to perceive that Bravo's behaviour was probably due to the effect of the poison. 'I'm not surprised Mr Bravo didn't ask me about the cause of his illness,' said Dr Johnson. 'A person as ill as that is perfectly indifferent to most things.'

Even Sir William Gull agreed:

Q: Is it possible for a man to be so ill that, although his mind is
      perfectly clear, he feels indifferent to everything, even his own
      life, as with sea-sickness?
A: I think it is likely.

Q: Is that the kind of state that antimony produces?
A: I think it is likely.

A further clue to Bravo's reactions lies in the text of an essay that I unearthed, written for the *Lancet* magazine in 1876. In the essay Dr Johnson describes his treatment of Bravo's abdominal pain: 'We agreed to give the patient morphia,' he said, 'as often as it might be necessary.'

We don't know how much morphine was administered to Charles Bravo through the fifty-five hours of his illness. But it was likely to have been a considerable amount. Dr Johnson said his patient suffered 'an agonizing death'. Dr Moore recalled how Bravo had 'screamed with pain many times.'

Morphine, of course, is an alkaloid derivative of opium, one of the most powerful narcotics known to man. Its mind-altering properties are well established. The effect of morphine on Bravo's mental state must also explain why he was so ambivalent to the things he was told.

So let us review the evidence. We know that Charles Bravo had no reason to take his own life; in fact he was 'a very ambitious man, with every reason to live.' We now know that he had studied medical jurisprudence and would not have used antimony as a means of killing himself. Furthermore my experiments at the Priory have discredited Mrs Cox's account of his 'confession'. And we have also established that his perplexing behaviour during his illness can be explained simply with reference to his neurological condition.

But there remains a final footnote. Why did Sir William Gull staunchly insist that Bravo had poisoned himself, even to the extent of being isolated from his professional colleagues and ridiculed in court? Was he really convinced that Bravo had committed suicide? Or was there something else?

Interestingly, Sir William Gull has recently been exposed as a high-ranking Freemason. Studies of this secret organization have revealed that, in the nineteenth century, its members were compelled to act or speak in a manner that benefited fellow Masons. The great industrialist who owned Buscot Park, who had been a High Sheriff of Berkshire – and whose daughter was suspected of murder – would probably also have been a high-ranking Freemason.

But Joseph Bravo, the stepfather to the dead man, and an immigrant West Indian Jew, would not.

CHAPTER TEN

Not Murder, Manslaughter

It is possible that Florence had not intended to kill Charles, but only to make him too ill to attempt to make love with her . . . It is possible that Florence mistakenly used a more potent dose of the substance than she intended.

PROFESSOR MARY HARTMAN, Rutgers University

Professor Mary Hartman was a renowned academic who had made a lengthy study of the Bravo case, beginning in the late 1970s. She was Professor of History at Rutgers University in the United States, and had researched a dozen well-known murder cases involving Victorian women. Her conclusions about the death of Charles Bravo were startlingly original, and had become fashionable in the academic world. A major BBC documentary on the case, called *An Infamous Address*, had also endorsed her conclusions.

In the autumn of 1999 I finally traced Professor Hartman, now Director of the Women's Studies Institute at Rutgers University, in New Jersey, and asked her during a long interview to develop her theory further. She was charming and informative about her work, and eager to discuss all aspects of the story.

Professor Hartman believed that Bravo's death was not murder at all, but a tragic accident. She believed that Florence had been unbalanced by the prospect of another pregnancy and miscarriage, and that she had taken steps to restrict Charles's intimate contact with her. On the night he was poisoned, she argued, Florence had gone into his room with a sachet of antimony and slipped some into his drink – not to kill him, but simply to render him too ill to make love to her. In her drunken state, however, Florence had tipped too much emetic into the water, killing her husband by accident.

Was Professor Hartman right? Did this theory account for the events at the Priory? 'I believe that Florence was frightened her husband would come to her room and force her to have sex,' said the Professor. 'In her desperation she tipped some antimony into his water jug. But she had been drinking. And when she shook the crystals out of the packet she accidentally fouled the jug with a fatal overdose.' She added: 'We know that Florence had been grievously ill with two miscarriages, and that she was desperate to avoid a third pregnancy, which might well have killed her. We also know that Bravo had shown little sign of agreeing to abstain from sex. He wanted his conjugal rights and he wanted children.'

Professor Hartman's ideas sprang partly from historical knowledge of her subject, and partly from intuition. Historically, there was a widespread belief that many middle-class Victorian women were in the habit of putting chemicals like antimony into their husbands' wine or water as a means of forestalling their sexual demands. Contraceptives were not widely available, it was argued. For women who were anxious not to have more children, and whose husbands refused to confine sexual activity to the menstrual cycle, it was necessary to resort to other, surreptitious means of birth control.

Professor Hartman was also able to point to contemporary evidence to support this theory. In 1885 – nine years after the Bravo case – a young woman named Adelaide Bartlett was charged with using chloroform to murder her husband. When she was asked to explain why she had been buying large quantities of the poison prior to his death, she claimed that she had been sprinkling it onto his handkerchief to make him too drowsy for sex. Her explanation seemed to strike a popular chord with many women reading her evidence.

'But the thing that really convinced me that Charles's death was an accident,' said the Professor, 'was Florence's reaction to it all. She was struck dumb by what had happened. She became hysterical. And none of the doctors thought that she was acting. They thought her reactions were absolutely genuine.'

Here again Professor Hartman was substantially correct. 'Her behaviour seemed quite natural and real,' said Dr Harrison. 'I saw no acting in her conduct,' said Dr Moore. The butler recalled in his evidence how Florence had come screaming down the corridor at the Priory, shouting for help: 'She said, "Get someone, Rowe! I don't care who it is – get anyone!" She screamed it at me,' he said. Even the Crown counsel at the inquest said that her behaviour was 'generally consistent with innocence'. Having found that her husband was dying, and that she was responsible, Florence would have had no choice but to let the illness take its course. In more progressive times, perhaps, she might have pleaded guilty to manslaughter.

Professor Hartman's theory intrigued me for a long time. It certainly resolved many of the most puzzling elements of the story. It explained, for instance, why Mrs Cox lied to the doctors (assuming, as one must, that she knew the truth). It also accounted for Florence's shock when she was confronted with a husband who was half dead.

And Professor Hartman was not alone in her view. Some days after speaking to her, I also contacted the writer and novelist, Elizabeth Jenkins, now living in retirement in Hampstead. She had written one of the first full-length books on the case, and had studied it over a forty-year period. Miss Jenkins said: 'Since I first wrote about the case in 1949 I have learned a great deal more about the matter – and I don't altogether hold the view of it that I once did. I assumed that the murder had been committed by Mrs Cox. But in this century a more modern alternative has presented itself.

'Florence had had two miscarriages. In the nineteenth century a device sometimes resorted to by women to postpone pregnancy was to administer an emetic to make the husband sick. I subscribe to the theory that, with Mrs Cox's connivance, she doctored the water bottle with a dose that she meant to incapacitate him. It was only when Mrs Cox found him that the dreadful consequences were brought home. Florence was much too frightened to admit what she had done. In their frantic attempts to protect themselves from a capital charge, she and Mrs Cox then claimed that Charles had committed suicide.'

Over the next few weeks I set about testing this theory. I interviewed several academics, in order to assess the socio-historical evidence for this unusual form of birth control. But the reactions were mixed, and most people were highly sceptical. Professor James Walvin, an expert in Victorian social history at the University of York, expressed amusement when I suggested to him that Charles Bravo had met his end in this manner. And when I conducted my own researches, at the library of the Wellcome Institute of the History of Medicine, I was able to find no hard evidence to support the claim that Victorian women employed these methods to avoid pregnancy. I also looked over the transcripts of the Bartlett case, which showed quite clearly that Adelaide had actually got off the charge of murdering her husband because of her clever counsel, not because of any plausible defence. The judge, jury, and witnesses at her trial all expressed incredulity at her alleged reason for wanting chloroform. Indeed, one of the medical witnesses said: 'The idea that women sprinkle poison onto their husbands' handkerchiefs in order to ward off unwelcome attention only exists in novels.'

Another damning argument against the manslaughter theory was evidential: Bravo certainly *did* want to resume sexual relations with his wife. Professor Hartman was right about that. He had no understanding of Florence's need to recuperate slowly from her illness. Nor did he appreciate how much it had affected her. But it is also clear that *he did not intend to sleep with her on the night he was poisoned*. That night he retired to his own room. He allowed Mrs Cox to sleep with his wife. The fact that he took a drink of water shows that he intended to remain in his own room for the rest of the evening, since this was always the last thing that he did before going to sleep. In addition, Bravo also knew that Florence had had her busiest day for many weeks, and would be much too weary for sex. She had been to London – her first outing for some time – and she had taken dinner downstairs – her first formal meal. So it was implausible to suggest that he was going to burst into the master bedroom, haul Mrs Cox from the bed, and then proceed to force himself on his exhausted wife. In these circumstances there was no reason why Florence might have felt threatened that night, and no reason for her to resort to an emetic.

But my strongest doubt about this theory was the obvious one: I found it impossible to believe that Florence had managed to pollute her husband's water jug with forty grains of antimony when her intention was to deposit just two or three grains into it. It was no use pretending that Florence did not know the effects of antimony. She was a clever and astute woman. She would not risk administering an emetic to her husband without establishing how much should be given. She would know that forty grains of antimony was about ten times the fatal dose. Of course it can be argued that Florence was drunk when she crept into Charles's room. That cannot be ruled out. But it remains unlikely. We know that Florence was not incapacitated by alcohol, that she was able to talk coherently to the staff, including the butler and the maid. It must also be remembered that anyone trying to poison their partner's drink with a substance that was usually fatal – even in tiny doses – would take very great care as they dropped the crystals into the water. The gravity of the task would itself have a sobering effect, and concentrate even the drowsiest mind.

It was true that one could *almost* make out a case for the manslaughter of Charles Bravo, a case in which a sick wife struggled to keep her lascivious husband at bay. One could *almost* go along with an idea like that. Yet those fundamental problems remained. Nothing explained why Florence felt threatened that night, with Charles safely tucked up in bed; nor how she had managed to tip such a massive dose of poison into her husband's water jug.

CHAPTER ELEVEN

Upstairs, Downstairs

Name and Quantity of Poison – 2 oz. Emetic Tartar
Purpose for which required – Horse Medicine
Signature of Purchaser – G. Griffiths
Sale of Poisons Register, Smiths, Streatham

'I wouldn't like to be in his shoes. He'll be dead in a few months.' These were the parting words delivered by George Griffiths, Florence's coachman, in the Bedford Hotel, exactly four months before Charles Bravo's death. Was it a coincidence? Was it second sight? Or perhaps a clue to a premeditated plan of murder?

The train of events that had so violently provoked George Griffiths was well documented; he had been dismissed by Bravo in the winter of 1875. The dismissal was especially hard because he had recently married and his young wife was expecting a baby. Then Bravo had evicted them from the little cottage that belonged to Florence. It had become clear during his inquest testimony that Griffiths bore a considerable grudge against his former employer. And Griffiths was the purchaser of antimony. The records of the local chemist revealed that he had bought four ounces of tartar emetic the previous autumn. But had Griffiths murdered Bravo? Could a bitter grievance really have driven him to kill a man he hardly knew?

The police files reveal that Inspector Clarke had finally traced Griffiths to a house in Herne Bay, Kent, two weeks after the murder. The house belonged to Lady Prescott, who employed him as her coachman. The interview with Griffiths had been conducted by Detective Sergeant Andrews, who had described his subject as a 'surly and difficult man'. Andrews had also spoken to the landlord of the Bedford, who'd reported his conversation with Griffiths some months earlier. 'I remembered it because it was so strange,' the landlord had said. 'He was very put out at losing his job and he blamed Mr Bravo.'

The police report of the interview with Griffiths made interesting reading. Faced with two officers in the drawing room of Lady Prescott's house, the coachman's blistering resentment at his old employer appears to have evaporated. 'It was just words,' he said. 'I looked on Mr Bravo as having got me out of my place. I should still be working there now if it wasn't for him.' Was it true that Griffiths had said that Bravo wouldn't live for very long, that he had told the manager of the hotel that Bravo was going to die? Griffiths replied that it was true. But the remarks had had nothing to do with poisoning Mr Bravo. Bravo had been bitten by a dog, Griffiths explained, some weeks before the wedding. The doctor had been called. People were concerned about hydrophobia. In the end Mrs Bravo had had the animal put down. 'I was thinking he might die from the dog bite,' Griffiths explained, good-naturedly.

Inspector Clarke's instinct was to exonerate Griffiths. He was a 'strange' character but he was 'no murderer'. Although he had lost his home and his job he was a skilled horseman, whose trade was always in demand. He had found employment in Herne Bay within three days of being sacked. 'It didn't matter to me whether he was dead or alive,' Griffiths had said. 'I had somewhere else to go for my living.' 'He seems to have put the matter behind him,' Clarke noted. And there was another reason for doubt, an insurmountable problem in fact. The coachman had told Inspector Clarke that he had been in Kent, working in the stables, at the time of Bravo's death. Lady Prescott had vouched for him and had even offered to sign a statement to that effect. So Griffiths would have required an accomplice if he had planned to kill Bravo. It was true that he had remained friendly with the butler at the Priory – both men agreed on that – but it was outside the realms of credibility to suggest that Griffiths could have persuaded him to carry out a murder merely to settle the score over his dismissal.

But what of the other servants at the Priory – the stable hands, gardeners and footmen? What of Mary Ann and the butler, Rowe? Again, it seems that Clarke was satisfied that he could rule them out. The gardeners and stable hands had all enjoyed access to the antimony. But none of them could have got to Bravo's bedroom on that fatal night without being detected. Mary Ann had filled up the water jug. The butler had run Bravo's bath. But both Rowe and Mary Ann would have looked incongruous rummaging around in the coachman's cupboard for a sachet of crystals. And even if they *had* managed to obtain antimony, and deposit it in the water jug, neither of them had a motive for murder. Neither of them stood to benefit from Bravo's death.

To a great extent we are dependent on George Clarke's powers of deduction in scrutinizing the staff at the Priory. That is an uneasy position in which to find oneself, since his record during this investigation was not exactly exemplary. But he explains his reasoning throughout, and appears to have persuaded both his own commanding officer and the Home Secretary that he had no grounds for suspicion. 'I am satisfied that none of Mrs Bravo's servants,' he wrote, 'were involved in what happened.'

CHAPTER TWELVE

Above Suspicion

I think it was Dr Gully who killed Charles Bravo. I've always felt he was the only person who had an overwhelming motive and who was the right type: exceedingly competent, successful, and always considered above suspicion. None of the other suspects is in the least credible.

AGATHA CHRISTIE, *Sunday Times*, October 1968

As soon as James Gully heard about Charles Bravo's death he had been waiting for the police to arrive. There would be an inquiry. The gossip in Balham would reach Scotland Yard. And the ruinous scandal that Gully and Florence had fought off three years earlier, when Gully had taken his Gladstone bag and his bottles of liniment up to the Priory, would come anyway.

In the end it was not a local gossip who breached Gully's defences, but a letter written anonymously about him to *The Times*. The letter had a Malvern postmark and its implications were clear: James Gully had been abandoned by his former mistress and had never got over it. After she had married Bravo, he had written a series of anonymous letters to her husband, outlining their affair, hoping that it would break up the marriage. When that failed he had decided to eliminate his young rival. He had inveigled Mrs Cox into carrying out the murder – knowing that she also had a motive for getting rid of Bravo – and had arranged for a bottle of antimony tartrate to be delivered to her house. 'They were seen together many times in Balham,' said the letter. 'And this, after he had said that he would never speak to her again.'

At first, George Clarke had barely bothered to consider the possibility. It seemed extraordinary to imagine that these two people could have arranged a murder pact – one motivated by money, the other by revenge. But then – as Clarke admitted in his first report – there was nothing remotely ordinary about Bravo's bizarre death. Gully was a physician and had spent his life trying to save lives. But he had also shown a ruthless streak in his dismissal of Alexander Ricardo. No one would have guessed that the sixty-seven-year-old therapist would be capable of seducing a female patient less than half his age. But that had happened, too. Clarke knew that James Gully had been angered by Mrs Bravo's rejection of him. The servants had told him that. He also knew that Bravo himself had felt haunted by the old man, and believed that Gully was trying to wreck his marriage.

The call came just after lunch on the afternoon of Friday, 29 May. The door was opened by Pritchard, who showed the Inspector into the drawing room. A contemporary photograph of Gully at his desk shows a sparsely furnished room in bold colours. There were photographs of the pump rooms at Malvern on the wall and framed copies of the architect's designs for the Hydro. There were also many prints of rare and wild flowers. Over the fireplace there were copies of embossed medical certificates from L'Ecole de St Barbe and L'Ecole de Médecine.

In my effort to prove James Gully's innocence, I travelled to Malvern to find out what I could about the man who had given it so much of its modern character, and to gauge the view of those who had researched and written about his role in the story of Charles Bravo.

As we've seen, members of Gully's own family couldn't even bring themselves to answer my request for an interview. My phone calls and letters met an implacable wall of silence. But at Malvern, where memorials to Dr Gully were dotted about, and the town's library had a vast collection of his papers and notes, there was a much greater sense of enthusiasm about the past. Students of Gully's life and work were keen to talk about him and to discuss the case. I contacted the Deputy Editor of the *Malvern Gazette* and spoke to reporters on the paper. I also contacted Dr John Harcup, a local GP with a strong interest in hydrotherapy, who had written a book about Gully, and spoke to the crime writer, Richard Whittington Egan, who lived in the town, in the aptly named Bravo House. I also spoke to Bill Howard, a local historian, who had strong views about Gully's role in Bravo's death.

I was never convinced by the popular image of Gully as the scorned lover, seething with thoughts of revenge. I believed that he understood clearly that Florence had made her choice, that the affair was over, and that the moment had come to close that chapter of his life. There could be no hope of regaining her, with or without Charles Bravo around. In his evidence at the inquest, Gully's butler had painted a lasting picture of a man resigned to the inevitable: 'He returned Mrs Ricardo's front door key to her,' he said. 'We watched the wedding procession going past the house. He expressed the hope that she would be happy.'

Gully's own evidence at the inquiry was also compelling:

'Did you bear a grudge against Mr Bravo?'

'I did not bear him a grudge. Not at all.'

'Did you write anonymous letters to him?'

'I have never written an anonymous letter in my life.'

'Were you still in love with Mrs Bravo at the time of her marriage?'

'I had strong feelings for her. But she had made up her mind whom she wished to marry.'

'Did you return her front door key to her?'

'I did.'

'Did you communicate with her after her marriage?'

'No.'

'Did you communicate with anyone from the Priory?'

'Only Mrs Cox.'

'It has been proved that you saw Mrs Cox five times in March and April.'

'That is true. But it was entirely accidental.'

'Did you give Mrs Cox a bottle of liquid?'

'I did.'

'Why did you not send the bottle straight to the Priory? Why did you send it to Mrs Cox?'

'Because I regarded all communication with the Priory as forbidden me.'

'Did you put tartar emetic into the bottle which you gave Mrs Cox?'

'I had no tartar emetic to place in the bottle. And any suggestion that I did so, from whatever quarter it may come, is a wicked and infamous falsehood.'

'Have you ever used antimony, in your professional capacity?'

'Not for thirty years, not since I went to Malvern. I have not had a grain of it in my possession since 1842.'

'Did you have anything to do with the death of young Charles Bravo, either directly or indirectly?'

'Upon my solemn oath I declare that I had nothing to do with Mr Bravo's death, either directly or indirectly.'

It was a convincing rebuke, firm and forensic. Though the public remained sceptical, it had been enough to convince a hostile jury of Gully's innocence.

But I was also strongly sceptical about the doctor's capacity for murder. It is one thing to lash out, rashly and blindly, in the heat of the moment; to commit a *crime passionnel* when the emotional threads of love, jealousy and betrayal suddenly and unexpectedly converge. It is another thing entirely to sit alone and cold-bloodedly plan an execution. I never for a moment believed that Gully was capable of either reaction.

These were, admittedly, sentimental reasons for arguing his innocence. But my visit to Malvern confirmed my belief that he was one of nature's altruists, incapable of the crime with which he was charged. I discovered that Gully had founded Worcestershire's first Co-Operative Society. He had donated to the poor. He had set up medical charities. I also discovered that he had become chairman of the local council. Everywhere I looked, I found public memorials enshrining his philanthropic character. Cora Weaver, a local historian, told me that when Gully had recovered from a serious illness in 1863, the entire population of the town threw a party to celebrate, parading through the streets, and finishing with an address at his front door. Under these circumstances it seemed ridiculous to believe that he was behind Bravo's death.

Yet it was not until I spoke to members of the Campbell family that I came across the evidence which, in my opinion, incontrovertibly cleared Gully of murder. Their assertions were, I later discovered, supported by a statement given to the Treasury Solicitor, and now part of the Home Office files, by Florence herself.

The Campbells said that Florence had arranged to see Dr Gully secretly soon after their affair ended. She was gripped by growing doubts about Charles Bravo's real reasons for pursuing her – her fear that he was after her money. She admitted in her Treasury statement how – unable to decide on the best course of action – she had sent a note to Gully, asking him to meet her in private at the Lower Lodge of the Priory, an empty stone cottage, formerly occupied by her groundsman. She had implored Gully to keep the meeting secret since she had already promised Charles that she would 'never see his face again'. Dr Gully duly arrived. It was six-thirty on a winter evening. Florence hadn't seen him since that day in Brighton when she had told him that their romance was over. Now, she said, she was desperate for his advice. She explained her doubts to him and Gully listened patiently. When she had finished he told her that she should be prepared to sign over to her fiancé the lease of the Priory, the carriages, the furnishings – everything except her inheritance from Alexander. She should give him what he demanded. 'It is a small price to pay,' he said, 'for your happiness.'

At the end of the discussion, she added, Gully had kissed her hand. He had thanked her for the pleasure she had brought into his life and expressed the hope that she would always be content. He was glad that they had had the opportunity to meet again and to part from each other on good terms. Then he had left. They were never to meet again.

Florence's evidence was vital, since it showed quite clearly that

Gully had come to terms with her desertion. He steadied her nerves just as she was about to break off her engagement to Charles. Had Gully been obsessed with his former mistress, as some claimed, and desperate to keep her, he would obviously have used this opportunity to persuade her to end her relationship. A single word from him would probably have been enough. Instead, he was to become the architect of the very marriage he was said to have loathed.

But if Dr Gully was not behind Bravo's death, there were two puzzles that I needed to resolve. Who had written the anonymous letters? And why had he had all those meetings with Mrs Cox just before Bravo's death?

The author of the letters was never traced. But it was unlikely to have been Gully. Such an action would have been entirely out of character. And Gully's own denial – 'I have never written an anonymous letter in my life' – rings true. Yet *someone* connected to the couple bore Bravo a grudge. And as I looked back over the events of that Christmas an obvious candidate emerged: good old George Griffiths.

What better way was there for the former employee to get back at the man who had wrecked his cosy life at the Priory? 'I should still be working there now,' Griffiths had said, at the inquest, 'if it wasn't for him.' Griffiths knew all about the sexual liaison between Gully and Florence. He had worked for Gully in Malvern. He had seen them together, driven them around on numerous occasions. And he had gossiped with all the other members of staff. He was the only person connected to Charles and Florence who would have been in a position to reveal privileged details of the affair.

The timing of the correspondence also suggests George Griffiths. The rift between Florence and Gully had taken place in November. Yet the anonymous letters didn't appear until Christmas. Griffiths had been sacked just before Christmas. And it was after he had left for his new job in Kent that the letters dried up.

The meetings with Mrs Cox, however, were more puzzling. Were the couple discussing ways of helping Florence as her marriage disintegrated? Was Gully taking a paternalistic interest in his former lover even though their affair was over? He obviously still cared for her. Perhaps Mrs Cox was meeting him once a week to ask for his advice on managing Charles Bravo's impossible temper? Yet the more I thought about it, the more I considered that the answer was much more prosaic; the string of meetings, I believed, were actually nothing more than a coincidence.

For the police, it was impossible to accept that such contact could occur by chance. The prevailing will was to find a pattern, a reason for suspicion, in the blind chain of events. But coincidences abound, and the Bravo story is full of them. The family of James Gully, for instance, owned coffee plantations near Kingston, Jamaica, while Charles Bravo's family had originated in Kingston and had made their money from exporting the coffee grown by Gully's grand-parents. Later, the Bravos had moved to St Ann's Bay, which eventually became the home of Mrs Cox and her children. After he had arrived in Malvern, Gully went to live in a house called the Priory, in Church Road. The house that Florence leased in Balham was called the Priory. Another resident of Church Road was Mortimer Ricardo, a relative of Alexander. During the inquest, Bravo's best friend told the court that he had been to school with Florence's younger brother – who had also been treated by James Gully. Meanwhile Mrs Cox's lawyer, Sir Reginald Bray, consulted a fellow barrister, Arthur Channell. Channell had been at Oxford with Bravo. And Bray had a relative who lived in Malvern. The people and the places are replicated, randomly and without meaning.

There is no doubt that the Bravo case ruined James Gully. *Punch* magazine drew a caricature-grotesque of him as an oily, half-human monster, with a dripping tap instead of a nose. By the time he entered the courtroom public opinion was so strongly against the doctor that the jury baulked at the idea that he should be allowed to sit down. 'The privilege of sitting down during evidence is reserved for women only,' said the foreman.

In the end, Gully survived his mistress by five years. He remained at Orwell Lodge, supported by his spinster sisters, and by Pritchard, but ostracized by his daughter, Susanna. He was blackballed from several of the clubs and institutions that had so enthusiastically welcomed his patronage at the height of his fame. After his death, on 15 March 1883, the gradual decline of Malvern became inexorable. His business partner had died some years earlier, and although the hydrotherapy clinics continued to treat patients, none of the handful of physicians who ran them was able to attract the interest originally generated by their charismatic founder. The last patient left the remaining clinic in the summer of 1913, and in the same year the only surviving hydrotherapist, Dr N. F. Ferguson, was declared bankrupt.

CHAPTER THIRTEEN

'A Good Little Woman'

An article as necessary to a Lady as her brougham or her bouquet is her Companion. Even those who are so bold that they could face anything, dare not face the world without a female friend.

WILLIAM THACKERAY, *Vanity Fair*

Mrs Cox has got herself into a great deal of trouble for not telling the truth.

FREDERICK ROWE, Florence Bravo's butler, quoted in the *Daily Telegraph*, 12 August 1876

By now, Mrs Cox was in focus, gravitating to the heart of the mystery. When the jury returned their verdict of murder – dismissing her story that Charles had confessed to suicide – they were indicting Jane Cox more strongly than anyone else in the house. But were they right to do so?

Jane Cox's motive for murder was perhaps the strongest of all the suspects'. She had three sons to support. She had no resources of her own. She had a mortgage. She owed money. At this critical moment Charles Bravo intervened to dismiss her. Bravo said she was an unnecessary expense. He could also sense how close his wife was to her, and the subliminal influence that she exerted over Florence. By the time of his death, the tensions in the marriage were so strong that the friendship between the two women amounted to a virtual conspiracy.

If Bravo had lived long enough to carry out his threat, then Mrs Cox would have found herself in a desperate situation. She paid no rent at the Priory. Her meals were provided. Her living costs were nil. Because of this she was able to let the house where she would normally have lived and pay off her mortgage through the rent she charged. Bravo's plans therefore attacked her at the most fundamental level.

For this reason a formidable body of opinion had come to endorse 'the economic motive', as it was called. 'She disliked the notion of leaving a comfortable house,' one newspaper wrote, after the inquest, 'and may have had a grudge against Bravo as the cause of her removal.' Sir John Hall, in his book on the case, said: 'Mr Bravo fully intended to dispense with Mrs Cox's services and he was not a man to be easily turned from his purpose. In these circumstances Mrs Cox had much to gain by his death.'

'She had her children to maintain,' wrote *The Times*, in 1920, 'and that provided the strongest of motives.'

'In her situation,' wrote Bernard Taylor, the author of a recent book on the case, 'there can be no doubt that Mrs Cox must have felt a growing hatred for Charles Bravo . . . What would become of her sons when she had been dismissed from her well-paid position at the Priory, and no longer had any home to go to? Clearly, something would have to be done.'

But motive alone was not sufficient to carry an indictment. The police knew that. What else was there? One afternoon in the New Year, a month or so into my research, I spent the afternoon at the British Library, going through the newspaper reports of Mrs Cox's inquest testimony. She had been in the witness box for two days and there was a mountain of evidence, all of it reported verbatim. (It is hard for us to grasp nowadays, where even the most sensational cases are summarized, but in 1876 reporters published almost everything uttered by a witness.)

The physicians who had attended Bravo had spoken vaguely of their dissatisfaction with Mrs Cox, and with her actions on the fatal night. But they had not voiced any specific complaints. Going over the evidence again, one was able to pinpoint exactly where the companion had slipped up. I made a list of six points in my notebook:

First, there was Mrs Cox's account of her response to Charles Bravo's cry for help. She told the inquiry that she had been in Florence's bedroom when she had heard Bravo shout from the landing. She had also said that to the police. 'She told me that she heard him cry out very loudly,' recalled Inspector Clarke. The doctors had agreed: 'Mrs Cox told me she heard Mr Bravo calling out,' said Dr Moore. As a result, she said, she had gone to his assistance.

But the court had failed to spot a critical discrepancy in Mrs Cox's evidence. The account of events given by Mary Ann Keeber – a highly convincing witness – directly challenged Mrs Cox's statement. The maid said that she had been going down the stairs when Charles had called out from the landing, *and that there had been no response to his cries from Florence's bedroom*. When she had entered the bedroom, she said, she had found Mrs Cox 'just sitting there, beside the bed.'

This is a deeply devastating statement for Mrs Cox to deal with. Having claimed that she had reacted to Bravo's cries, she found herself flatly contradicted by an independent witness who said that she had done nothing. Florence at least could blame her inertia on the amount of alcohol she had drunk – but Jane Cox couldn't. Mary Ann said that Mrs Cox had been sitting on her stool, knitting, ignoring the shouting that was going on outside.

This point was further underlined during my visit to the Priory. Here I was able to establish beyond doubt that Mrs Cox would certainly have heard Charles Bravo cry out from the landing.

The first thing that hits you as you mount the stairs in the Priory is how small everything seems. The overwhelming sensation is one of compression. The door from which Charles Bravo emerged to call out that night is no more than a few feet from the top of the stairs. And how far is it from Florence's room? During my visit there I measured the distance at just over four feet. Assuming that Charles had taken two or three paces from his bedroom door onto the landing, as Mary Ann said – which would have taken him to the lip of the stairs – he was then about four and a half feet from the door of Florence's bedroom. Mary Ann Keeber remembered that Charles called out very loudly. In fact her words were: 'He called out as loudly as he could.' Over a distance of four feet, therefore, *there is no conceivable way in which Mrs Cox could have failed to hear his voice.* And yet she did nothing. She stayed where she was, rooted to her seat.

Why had Mrs Cox ignored Charles's cry? As the poisoner, she would have had everything to gain by leaving it unanswered, and she would have had a great deal to lose by raising the alarm. Once the alarm was raised, then there would be an attempt to revive him. The effect of the poison would be delayed. Doctors would be summoned. Charles might even recover. But if things were left to run their course, then he would quickly slip into unconsciousness. He would either choke to death on his own vomit or die from the effects of the poison.

This was the first clear evidence of deceit by Mrs Cox. Yet the police, the Coroner and the lawyers had failed to notice it.

The second point that I recorded concerned Mrs Cox's decision to delay sending for help. She did this by sending for Dr Harrison, who lived several miles away, instead of Dr Moore, who lived in Balham High Street. If Florence hadn't intervened, and cut through her delaying tactics, Charles would have been deprived of proper medical attention for well over an hour. In her inquest testimony Mrs Cox tried to justify this by saying that Dr Harrison was the *family* physician, and that she did not want to admit to a local man that Charles had taken poison. But I found this immensely difficult to believe. For me, the idea that one risked a breach of privacy by sending for a local man – that he would afterwards tootle around the district, gossiping about the incident – seemed to deny medical ethics to the point of incredulity.

I also felt that anyone genuinely interested in the welfare of Charles Bravo would not have disregarded a local doctor: Charles's appearance confirmed the presence of a desperate illness. He had collapsed and vomited blood. His teeth had locked together. His pulse was barely detectable. When Mary Ann saw him she was so alarmed that she was unable to mix a mustard solution. She also took it upon herself to summon her mistress, a very strong indication of how ill Bravo must have looked. Even Florence, when alerted, ordered a local man. And Charles Bravo didn't simply *look* ill: according to Mrs Cox, he had actually *confessed* to swallowing poison. How likely was it, therefore, that anyone who knew this, and who wished to save his life, would have been concerned about the proprieties of sending for the 'right' doctor?

The third piece of evidence against Mrs Cox was her attempt to confuse the medical team. She offered the doctors a list of possible causes for his illness, even though she claimed later that Charles had already confessed to poisoning himself.

Fourth, there was Mrs Cox's curious reaction to Bravo's vomiting. What would be the instinctive reaction of someone who had just been told that an unconscious man had swallowed poison? It would surely be to preserve his vomit in order to establish what had been taken – and then effect an antidote. But this was not the instinctive reaction of Mrs Cox, a woman trained in sickroom procedures. All her efforts were directed towards *preventing* the physicians from taking samples of his vomit: she washed out the bowl into which Charles had been sick. And she failed to tell the doctors that Charles had vomited from the window. (Even when Dr Harrison asked her what had become of Bravo's vomit, *she didn't tell him that some of it was lying on the roof, a few feet beneath them.* 'I asked Mrs Cox for the vomit and she said it had been thrown away,' he recalled.)

Fifth, Mrs Cox had tried to prevent the physicians from finding out that Charles was bleeding internally. This would have hastened their diagnosis of an irritant poison. She changed his bloodstained nightshirt as he lay unconscious, and had it taken away by the maid and put into the laundry. It was never retrieved. And when Bravo passed a bloodied bowel motion in bed, in the presence of one of the physicians, she announced that Charles had been drinking large quantities of *red* burgundy at dinner!

Sixth, there was Mrs Cox's failure to send for a stomach pump. She could not plausibly claim that she did not realize that a stomach pump was needed. Her instructions to Mary Ann – to fetch mustard and water to make Bravo vomit – showed quite clearly that she knew that Bravo's stomach had to be flushed out. Yet, the trained night nurse, the former governess, who had made her living in domestic service, failed to send for the one instrument that might have saved the sick man's life.

A final point occurred to me as I left the Public Record Office in Kew and headed for the tube. I realized that the measures that Jane Cox employed to treat Charles Bravo were well-known measures for treating poison – mustard, hot water, coffee and camphor, all of which were designed to bring him round and make him vomit. This had to mean one of two things: either Bravo *had* told Mrs Cox that he had taken poison, as she claimed. Or she somehow knew it herself. Since I had already ruled out the possibility that Bravo had told her he had taken poison – because the maid did not hear him – I was left with the conclusion that Mrs Cox treated Bravo for poison because she knew that he had been poisoned *before she entered the bedroom.*

It was, overall, an extraordinary catalogue. When you sat it squarely beside her motive you could produce a case that seemed to prove Mrs Cox's guilt almost incontrovertibly. It was no wonder that so many people who had looked into the case had come away with the conclusion that she was the murderer. But what had happened to George Clarke? Why had he not analysed the details in the same way? Perhaps his own inquiries had reached a kind of critical mass, where the plethora of detail simply swamped the obvious conclusions.

But my research was still going on. Although I didn't know it then, rumbling back across London on the underground, a dramatic new discovery was about to be made 6,000 miles away that would wreck the whole edifice of my case against Jane Cox. I had thought she was guilty. I had almost been convinced. But she was innocent of Bravo's murder, and soon I would be able to prove it.

My quest for Mrs Cox had begun at the General Register Office, London. Here, after three days of searching, I discovered that she had died in London in 1917, aged ninety. She had been buried in Hither Green Cemetery and her last known address was Cambridge Road, Lee, a suburb of Lewisham. The informant of her death was her son, Henry, the youngest of her three boys, who had been living with her at the time. The cause of death was listed, somewhat characteristically, as 'exhaustion'.

I travelled to Lee on the outside chance that there might be descendants of Henry Cox still in the area. At the offices of Lewisham Council I searched for evidence that Henry had remained in the area after his mother's death. But he was not buried at Hither Green, nor were either of his brothers. I contacted all the residents of Lee with the same surname, using that old friend of the modern journalist, the telephone directory. But none of them was related to Jane's family, and none of the older residents of the area to whom I spoke could remember the Cox family. For the moment, it seemed, the trail had gone cold.

At this point I decided to approach the problem from another end. Instead of starting with Mrs Cox's death, I decided to return to the year of the crime and attempt to trace her movements from there. I knew – it was a wisp of memory – that one of the newspapers had reported her departure for the West Indies in October 1876, two months after the inquest ended. But nothing had been heard of her since then. In the late 1980s, the writer Bernard Taylor had made a concerted effort to establish what had happened to Mrs Cox, but his attempts had ended in failure. 'One wonders what became of her between the inquest and the time of her death,' he wrote. 'Our researches have revealed no answers.'

Somehow, I felt that these missing years between 1876 and 1917 were absolutely central to discovering whether or not Mrs Cox had murdered Charles Bravo. I felt sure that they contained some kind of key – a piece of physical evidence – which would resolve the whole question.

I began by looking up my old friend from undergraduate days, Professor James Walvin, a lecturer in history, who had taught for many years in the West Indies. Professor Walvin travelled annually to Jamaica to conduct research and to deliver lectures on Jamaican slavery. He knew the island well and had many friends there. I rang him and arranged to see him. The following day I was sitting in his office in Alcuin College, where he was Provost, the brilliant May sunshine cascading through the room, chatting over the intricacies of the story. He was, as usual, personable and keen to help, and was optimistic that there was fresh information waiting to be discovered. He suggested that I begin at the Jamaican National Library in Kingston, where there would be records of prominent landowners and civic leaders, at the Jamaica National Archives in Spanish Town, and in the Department of History at the University of the West Indies, where he would put me in touch with Patrick Bryan, the distinguished Head of Faculty. He gave me the names of several other contacts who would assist me with research, and spoke to a number of academics on my behalf. Soon afterwards I flew to Kingston, and journeyed later to St Ann's Bay, on the north of the island, to consult parish records and government archives. Within days, as a result, the whole shape of the story was to change.

Two days after my arrival in Jamaica I unearthed a series of documents from the Spanish Town record office relating to the Cox family. The documents showed that the family had lived five miles south of St Ann's Bay, and had owned three plantations there: Content, a pimento estate; Endeavour, where they grew coffee and tobacco; and Carlton, a vast tea plantation. Philip (Jane's husband) Cox's uncle, it transpired, was the Honourable Henry Cox, a celebrated West Indian politician, who had represented the parish of St Mary in the House of Assembly. *The Jamaica Almanac for 1821* listed him as one of only sixteen Assemblymen who owned 5,000 acres or more of plantation land, a figure that made the family one of the wealthiest on the island. Content, the family home, was one of the largest estates in Jamaica, encompassing over a thousand acres. Henry's wife, Margaret, was also a wealthy and powerful woman in her own right.

I imagined at first that this fine genealogical detail was of little relevance to the murder of Charles Bravo. The abstract layers of history were, I thought, of absorbing interesting to anyone as immersed in the story as I was, but of little value in the search for murder clues. But as I combed my way through the documents and gained a measure of the Cox family's tremendous wealth, I soon realized that the records did indeed have a direct bearing on the events of 1876. One document in particular proved to be decisive.

The records revealed that Henry Cox had died in 1855 and that Margaret Cox had died in 1879. They also revealed that the couple had had no children of their own. *So Margaret had decided that she would leave everything the family owned to her niece, Jane, and her three boys.*

Margaret, it seemed, had always been fond of Jane. She had supported her when Jane's husband had died. She had given her a generous financial settlement and had employed private tutors for her boys. She had also paid for her to return to London when Jane decided to leave Jamaica. She admired her niece's self-discipline and industry. Jane was not Margaret's only surviving family – there was another relative in Surrey – but she had become her favourite.

The papers confirmed that Jane had received her inheritance just over three years after Charles Bravo's death – indeed, I discovered that she and her sons were established in Jamaica, managing the estates, within six months of the Bravo inquest. The vital clue, however, was that *Mrs Cox had known that she and her children were due to inherit this fortune at the time of Charles Bravo's murder* – in fact, she had known it some two years before he died. Her alleged reason for killing Bravo, the famous 'economic motive', had therefore been incontrovertibly demolished.

In the spring of 1874, Mrs Cox had received a letter from her aunt, by then seriously ill, informing her that she had drawn up a new will, making Jane Cox and her eldest son, John, the beneficiaries of the family's fortune. I quote the correspondence in its entirety for the first time. The first letter is dated 26 March 1874:

My dear Jane,

 I think it right to let you know that I have left in my will all I have to John – Carlton, Content, cattle, horses, carriages, furniture and land &c, &c; and should I die before he comes of age you will not allow these properties to be sold, but carried on for his benefit. Mr Solomon and Mr John Sinclair are my executors, and I have no doubt that they will see every justice done. Some years ago I wrote to the Rev. John Cox [father of Philip] when he was living at Walgrave, [saying] that I would leave these properties to his three sons by his first wife, M. A. Woodward, but have long since revoked this, and I do not wish any of his family to have anything belonging to me. I never got anything from them. My own money paid for these properties and I can leave them to whom I please. You had better keep this to yourself; say nothing about it to anyone, not even John, while I am alive.

With much love,

Your affectionate aunt,

Margaret Cox

Over the course of the next eighteen months it appears that Margaret Cox's health worsened. She began writing to her niece regularly, urging her 'to come out as soon as possible', so that matters could be finalized. And there was a second reason why a visit was necessary: Margaret Cox was convinced that an unscrupulous banker would try to move into her property after her death if Jane did not appear in Jamaica. It was therefore vital that she sail as soon as she could. The second letter was sent on 8 May 1876 and the italics are Margaret's:

My dear Jane,

 Mr Solomon is going to America and is leaving all his business in the hands of the young man, Mr Chadwick, who you know is engaged to W. Stennett; and should anything happen to me [I think] they would get married and come here to live. No one has told me so, but I feel sure that would be the case. *Do not mention this to anyone. I really do think you ought to get out here as soon as possible.* I am not able now to attend to anything. *I am sure that were you to ask Mr Bravo he would pay your passage out, and when you wish to return*

144

Mr Solomon would do the same, and charge it to this property. Tell him this from me. I should like to see you again, and have many things to tell you which I cannot write about, so do come soon. Should you be able to manage this, do not bring John with you; it would be the ruin of him to come here so young. *Dora will tell you the rest.* I am not able to write more at present, but do come.

With much love,

Your affectionate aunt,

Margaret Cox

The news that Mrs Cox and her children were soon to inherit a vast fortune in the West Indies was an extraordinary turn of events for the companion. She had spent fifteen years struggling single-handedly to raise her children. And now she was being promised the kind of bursary that would make them secure for the rest of their lives. The court inventory of 1879 notes that the furnishings of Content included 'books, oloplates, chairs, beds and tables', worth around £150. Over £300 was being held by Joseph Bravo and Michael Solomon, and £30 was owed to the Estate by debtors. The physical assets at the house were worth £900 (ten times Mrs Cox's annual salary), and there were two more properties belonging to the family – Endeavour and Carlton. The total value of the inheritance lay in the region of £6,800 – a phenomenal sum for 1876.

In response to these letters, Jane Cox spoke to Joseph Bravo, who urged her to travel as quickly as possible. 'I agreed that I ought to go soon,' Mrs Cox said, later. Mrs Cox then composed a letter to her aunt, assisted by her friend, Mrs Harwood, confirming that she would sail as soon as arrangements had been made to look after her three boys. In due course, she spoke to Florence who agreed to take charge of the boys during the forthcoming school holidays.

In May, Mrs Cox received a letter from a neighbour of Margaret Cox (who was now too ill to write). She urged Jane to hurry.

Mrs Cox bids me tell you that she notes all you have said in your letter about coming out, and she hopes most earnestly that you will try to come out as soon as you can. It is very kind of Mrs Charles to promise to take care of the boys while you are away. I suppose it will make your mind more easy to think that they are with her while you are away. If you have not already left when you receive this, try and hasten out, for I know poor Mrs Cox wishes to see you.

These three letters in themselves support the assertion that Mrs Cox could not have been the murderer; Jane knew that she had to go quickly to Jamaica. Her position was under threat from the young man Chadwick, who was planning to move into one of the estates. She needed to assert her presence on the island. To have carried out a murder, with all the subsequent inquiries and delays, would have been entirely self-defeating. It would have kept her in England for months, putting her children's legacy at risk. No mother who exhibited the degree of Jane Cox's maternal devotion would have considered such a move.

But the real story here, amongst these dry and fragile papers, is the negation of Jane Cox's motive for murder. She and her children were to inherit a substantial fortune. They were set to enjoy the privileged lifestyle of the colonial aristocracy. Indeed, the Return of Properties for 1882 records them proudly surveying their land, masters of almost a thousand acres. And it is this document that exonerates Jane Cox from the charges against her. *Mrs Cox would never have killed Charles Bravo for financial reasons when she knew of her coming inheritance.*

The discovery of the Cox records, buried for over a century, represented one of those watershed moments in the investigation. They constituted that rare thing – a genuinely radical light on existing facts. Indeed, they served to change the whole picture of Bravo's death, and of the suspects who had orbited around him. A theory that had been accepted by investigators for over a century was suddenly stood on its head.

But how could we reconcile this new turn of events with the known evidence? Where does it leave us? It was clear that Jane Cox *had* lied to many people about Charles Bravo's murder. Her lies were there, in black and white, in the police file. But the new evidence also established that Mrs Cox had nothing to gain personally by Bravo's death. Her future was secure. So what had compelled her to fabricate evidence?

Who was she trying to protect? And why?

CHAPTER FOURTEEN

'Bitter Trouble'

My husband could be very cruel.

From the statement of Florence Bravo

Looking back on our ten weeks of marriage, I feel that many of my words to you . . . were unnecessarily harsh. In future my rebukes, if it be necessary to say anything, which God forbid, shall be given with the utmost gentleness. We have had bitter trouble, but I trust our lives will not be disturbed by memories like those.

CHARLES BRAVO, writing to his wife, 20 February 1876

We have returned to Florence. Florence Bravo had broken free of the net of suspicion that had first begun to close in around her at the inquest. The physicians who had attended her husband had described her reactions on the night of Bravo's death as 'perfectly natural'. For the Crown counsel, Sir Harry Poland, 'her behaviour was generally consistent with innocence.' *The Times* said that there was 'no evidence that Mrs Bravo had had any hand in her husband's strange death.' The indictment of the jury was against Mrs Cox, not Florence, who by then had convinced those in court that she was an innocent woman.

But was Florence innocent? Had the jury got it right? Almost certainly, they had not. The reason for Florence's acquittal had less to do with her innocence and more to do with the fact that the Crown had been unable to produce a plausible motive. But the motive for Charles Bravo's murder was there, staring at them from the pages of

Florence's inquest testimony and her police statement. For reasons that will become clear, the police were never attuned to the full significance of these documents. They also misunderstood a vital piece of evidence that allowed Florence to slip through the net. It is only now, with fresh evidence which I have discovered about her marriage to Charles, that we are able to see the reasons why Florence was compelled to commit murder. Furthermore, evidence that I have produced from the Wellcome Medical Library in London links Florence uniquely to the crime, through a previous acquaintance with the obscure poison that was used.

Florence's motive to commit murder was the same motive that compelled scores of women in her society to do away with their husbands – a disastrous marriage, from which there seemed to be no legitimate route of escape: Madeleine Smith, Florence Maybrick, Claire Reymond, Henriette Francey, Adelaide Bartlett. Time and time again, the social ethos of the period elicited the most strident remedies.

Florence's relationship with Charles Bravo has been only dimly understood. She had first met him in December 1875. She had embarked on a courtship so that she could regain the social respectability that she had lost through her affair with James Gully. Charles Bravo had seemed an ideal candidate – well educated, socially confident, and with a promising Parliamentary career in front of him. But Florence had begun to have second thoughts about her fiancé soon after the courtship had started. A copy of a letter that was given to me by one of Robert Campbell's descendants, dated 18 November, and written by Florence just after Bravo had proposed, throws new light on the state of their relations:

> After serious and deep consideration, I have come to the conclusion
> that if you still hope to gain my love then we must see more of each
> other, and be quite sure that the solemn act of marriage would be
> for the happiness of both of us . . . you have behaved in the noblest
> manner and I have no doubt of being happy with you, but of course
> before giving up my present freedom I must be quite convinced that

it would be for our mutual happiness. Whether we marry or
whether we do not, I shall ever have a great regard for you and take
a deep interest in your welfare.

This is an intriguing piece of evidence. The tone of the letter clearly
suggests that Florence was having doubts. She offered Bravo the
compensation of her friendship and her 'great regard'. But there was
no rush to marry. She had, at the very least, petitioned for a considerable delay while she considered her position.

Florence's unease stemmed from two things. First, she knew by
then that Bravo was marrying her for her money. That was why
she had insisted on invoking the Married Woman's Property Act.
Second, Florence suspected that she and Bravo were temperamen-
tally unsuited. It is noticeable that she mentions her own happiness
three times in one brief paragraph. She had evidently realized that a
man with Bravo's fossilized prejudices was ill-equipped to make
happy a woman of her unusually determined character. His coldness
and cynicism were probably attractive to Florence at first – they
echoed her own chilly personality – but she quickly grasped that
spending her life with such a person was a different matter to being
occasionally amused by them on a social level. Her great amour, after
all, was Gully: kind, considerate, supportive – the very antithesis of
Bravo's abrasive character. Subsequently, her letters to the man who
wanted to marry her are increasingly couched in indecision. In fact
it's almost possible to perceive the precise moment at which the tide
actually turned.

Yet less than one month after writing this letter, after pleading for
more time, Florence had married her fiancé. What had happened?
Unknown to the police or to the inquest lawyers, it seems that
Charles Bravo had forced Florence into marriage by getting her
pregnant. The evidence for this is very strong.

I had already discovered while researching the Bravo family that
the proposed wedding had been moved forward from the middle of
January to early December 1875. It was said at the time that this was
to enable Bravo's mother to attend the wedding, since she had a prior

engagement for the first date. But in the event Mrs Bravo still failed to attend. So the wedding must have been moved forward for other reasons. Florence's sudden discovery that she was pregnant would certainly explain this decision. But the strongest evidence lay within the extended family: I discovered that Charles Bravo's aunt, Emily Smith, had died at the end of November. Her funeral had taken place on 3 December. Victorian custom was unbending in responding to death; families mourned for much longer periods than is usual today, and all social events were banned until the designated period ended. *It is inconceivable that there would have been a wedding on 7 December – within a few days of a bereavement – unless there had been a very pressing reason for it.* The only plausible explanation was that Florence was already pregnant. It was, after all, on 9 January that she announced that she was expecting a baby.

This supposition is further supported by Florence's domestic servants, all of whom stated in their evidence that Charles had been staying nights at the Priory before his marriage. When asked to explain this, Florence said that his mother objected to him returning home at night 'as he took cold' – a claim so implausible that it was greeted with howls of derision in the Coroner's court. It should be remembered that Mrs Cox and Mary Ann both slept on the second floor at the Priory. Florence slept on the floor below. Charles slept in the guest room, the room where he later died. After the servants had gone up to bed there was nothing to stop him leaving his room and crossing the landing. If Florence had tried to refuse his sexual demands, Charles would have simply said that she had no right to deny her fiancé what she had already given to an illicit lover outside of marriage.

Again, the pregnancy had its roots in pragmatism. Bravo had intuited Florence's wish to retract from the engagement. Her decision to keep her money would have confirmed it. So he appears to have forced the marriage by placing her in an impossible position. Florence was trapped from the beginning. When she discovered her pregnancy she knew there was nothing to do but consent to the wedding. Her case history made another abortion out of the question.

In due course, Florence's anger at these tactics might have given way to less destructive feelings. Some couples do trap each other into marriage and the marriage survives. Had Charles Bravo been a different kind of man – supportive, loving, co-operative – then she might have found it possible to forgive him. But of course Bravo was not like that. And Florence's patience quickly evaporated. 'She does not appear to have had that love for him which he might have expected,' Chief Inspector Clarke had written. 'And she certainly shows no grief at his death.' Unwisely, the widow's grievances could not even be contained in the presence of the police.

We should now turn to the pages of Florence's testimony for the precise reasons why she decided to commit murder. Her first motive lay in the domestic life at the Priory, and in the 'ebullitions of temper' that Bravo inflicted on his new bride. What he could not win by charm, he would win by menace. In her police statement, Florence says that she first became aware of her husband's temper about two weeks after their wedding, when he exploded during a row over household management. Later he intimidated her with 'a violent tantrum'. On another occasion he stormed from the house and marched down the drive. Later he struck her a blow so hard that she fell to the ground. Florence's fear of Bravo was perhaps best exemplified by a scene that unfolded in the carriage on the morning of Bravo's illness. They quarrelled over James Gully and Bravo's face 'grew very dark'. 'I was frightened of him,' she recalled. 'He looked very violent.' Twelve hours later the poison had entered his system.

Charles Bravo's sexual proclivities presented a second problem in the marriage. Florence confided the shame she felt over the sexual activity that went on between the couple to her physician, Dr Dill. That shows how clearly the abuse had disturbed her. We have already seen how she guarded her right to dictate the sexual activity in her relationships. Here the very essence of her womanhood was being violated.

But neither of these problems would in themselves have been likely to produce a murder. They were the stock ingredients of a classically unhappy Victorian marriage, in which the wife learned to live with her personal misery, and saw it as the price of her own security. What pushed Florence over the edge was a much more fundamental problem.

Florence had become pregnant around the middle of November. She had lost the pregnancy two and a half months later, and was reported to be so ill that she couldn't even sit up in bed. Instead of a slow recuperation, however, she had to endure demands from her husband for the immediate resumption of his marital rights. So she was pregnant again in March. Once more she was unable to maintain the pregnancy. It was lost on 8 April. This time the results were calamitous. Physicians came and went. All of them expressed concern. One of them prescribed a long holiday. Florence retreated to her room, barring Bravo at the door. Mrs Cox went to the coast to find a house for her. But Bravo knew exactly what his wife was up to. And again the autocratic strain in his character asserted itself. Florence was 'a selfish pig'. Her convalescence was 'a useless expense'. She was trying to deprive him of what was rightfully his: a son and heir. She was over thirty; the years were marching on; there was no time to be lost on silly bouts of hypochondria.

It is difficult to overestimate the extent to which this situation must have affected Florence. Her letters are dominated by questions about her health. She needed care and understanding. Her mental state was at the mercy of a body shattered by miscarriages. She stayed in bed for nearly ten days, clinically depressed, unable to face anyone, taking her meals on a tray. And all the time her husband loomed in the doorway. By the time of the poisoning, Florence Bravo had come to believe that she was in mortal danger from Charles Bravo. And she could see no lawful way out of her predicament.

Some women would have met these problems with a controlled equanimity. But not Florence. As we've seen, Florence had come from a privileged background. She had been born into wealth. She had secured a fortune in her own right. She had, in short, an unshakeable belief in her own eugenic *entitlement* to happiness. By the time of her husband's murder this element of her personality was in revolt. She could no longer cope with the shame of sexual abuse, or the tyrannical rages, and she was unhinged by the prospect of another miscarriage. It was in these circumstances that she resolved to eliminate her husband.

Of course, at this point it has to be asked why Florence did not simply apply for a divorce or a legal separation. Murder was an extreme solution to her problems, however harrowing they were. But neither of these options was realistic for her. Divorce was impossible for a woman to obtain unless she could prove that a whole range of 'social crimes' had been committed against her – adultery, desertion, cruelty, the committing of 'an unnatural act'. It is impossible to find a single court case during this period in which a woman successfully sued her husband for divorce. A separation, on the other hand, might have been theoretically possible – had it required merely the consent of one partner. But the law in 1876 said that Charles Bravo also needed to agree to the move – something he would never have done. Bravo had worked hard to marry into money, and he was set on a public life, with all its proprieties and façades. He would never have tolerated the humiliation of a failed marriage. Of course Florence *could* have petitioned for a separation *without* his consent if she had been able to secure the support of a legal guardian. But no such man was available. Indeed, she later acknowledged that it was a 'miracle' that Gully had agreed to help her in 1870. Academic research has shown that many women tried to petition professional men for guardianship – particularly doctors and lawyers – but that the professions were governed by a strict code of practice forbidding involvement in private disputes.

In this climate – a misogynist's dream – Florence's options were narrow. Worse, the institutionalized order had itself become an inducement to breach the law.

How was it, then, that these issues had failed to come to the attention of the police at the time? How had Florence escaped arrest and indictment? The central reasons were simple. First, there was the key problem of evidence. In order to have convinced a jury of her motives for murder, the Crown would have required the testimony of independent witnesses. And independent witnesses eluded the police. The Bravo marriage had not been part of any interlocking social world – there were no eyewitness accounts of their relationship. The only people who *could* have substantiated the Crown's allegations were the domestic servants and Mrs Cox, all of whom had been prepared to lie on oath in order to protect their employer. The inability of the police to prise from the servants the kind of incriminating evidence that they undoubtedly possessed was their most costly failure.

Additionally, the one area where the Crown *might* have been able to make some progress was negated by the witness. Dr Charles Dill had reported Florence's experiences of anal intercourse to Chief Inspector Clarke. Yet Dill was never called by the Crown. And Florence was never properly cross-examined over the allegations she had made to him. It isn't clear why the Attorney General decided against using this evidence. The most likely explanation, however, is that Dr Dill had simply refused to testify against his patient, and that the Crown, unable to proceed without his evidence, had then decided against humiliating Florence in the witness box. The inquest was not a trial, after all.

But the biggest reason for the failure of the police inquiry was that the problems which Florence had experienced were *women's* problems. The police officers were all men. Their understanding of the effect of two miscarriages on Florence's mental health was limited by contemporary male ignorance of the physiology and physical experiences of women. They didn't understand what it meant to Florence – physically and psychologically – to have a man demanding that she bear his child when she was already acutely ill because of two failed pregnancies. It was strangely ironic that the ruling traditions of her society had both compelled her to act – and then saved her from the consequences.

Having established Florence's motives, we can now turn to the forensic and circumstantial evidence that incriminates her: the first of these is the use by the murderer of tartar emetic. This poison, as we shall see, bears Florence Bravo's hallmark in a unique way.

Twelve years before Charles Bravo's death, Florence had married Captain Alexander Ricardo, the Grenadier Guardsman. Ricardo was twenty-two and an alcoholic. Over the next seven years Florence tried to persuade her family to rescue her from a marriage in which she endured constant abuse at the hands of her husband. Their failure to do so provides us with the grounds for some interesting speculation.

As we have seen, this was a hard-drinking age. And one of its consequences was that women passed among themselves their encyclopaedic knowledge of the furtive methods that they could employ to control a husband's drinking: the slipping of substances into his beer or wine that would cause him to retch, and so – it was hoped – abstain; or, for the hopeless alcoholic, the administration of substances that would send him to sleep before his rages took hold.

During the course of my research I had already visited the Wellcome Medical Library, in Euston Road, London, to read up on the clinical details of antimony. Although I had found no evidence to support the idea that women used antimony as a method of birth control, there was certainly evidence that they used it *as a means of compelling their husbands to give up drinking*. A small amount of antimony, around a grain and a half, would be deposited in his wine in order to produce nausea.

This practice was actually referred to during the Coroner's inquest into Charles Bravo's death, when witnesses were asked about the contemporary uses of antimony. 'I have heard that ladies use tartar emetic to cure their husbands of drink,' Henry Smith had said. Smith was a surgeon at King's College Hospital. Professor Redwood, a chemist, had added: 'I know of cases where women put tartar emetic into wine to cure their husbands of their fondness for it.' Amazingly, however, no connection was made between the use of tartar emetic as a means of controlling alcoholism, Florence's previous marriage to an alcoholic, and the use of tartar emetic to poison Charles Bravo.

There can be no question, however, that Florence received advice from her female relatives about methods of controlling Alexander's drinking. At some point in her violent first marriage it is reasonable to suggest that Florence began to slip Alexander small doses of antimony. As a horsewoman she had unlimited access to it. And her use of the poison would explain the massive bouts of vomiting that Ricardo suffered before their separation: 'Up to sixty times a day,' according to Mrs Campbell. It would also explain the use of this most rare poison in the murder of Charles Bravo. Who else in that house would have known about the packets of antimony in the stables? And wouldn't the other suspects have employed poisons – like arsenic or strychnine – that were more easily administered? Potassium antimony tartrate had Florence's fingerprints all over it.

Having established her motives, and having linked her – uniquely in the household – with the use of antimony, the rest of the evidence against Florence Bravo falls easily into place. First, the timing of the murder points firmly towards Florence. Bravo was poisoned on the very day that his wife's convalescence officially ended. She was driven into town and she took her first meal downstairs. Normal life was returning to the Priory. Over dinner, Bravo made it clear that he expected to return to a routine sex life. He impatiently dismissed her recuperation in Worthing and threw down the photograph of the house she was renting. Three hours later, he was lying fatally poisoned.

Second, Florence was the only person with unlimited access to the poison that had been bought by George Griffiths – the purchase of antimony by anyone else would have been traced.

And Florence had the opportunity, too. She and Mrs Cox retired to bed before Bravo, and whilst the servants were eating. At the top of the stairs, she turned and sent Mrs Cox all the way down again for more wine. In that moment, she could easily have slipped into her husband's room, deposited the antimony into his water jug, and returned to the master bedroom before Mrs Cox reappeared. She claimed not to know that her husband drank water each night before going to bed. But that in itself gave a clue to her guilt.

There was no way she could *not* have known after four months of marriage.

Then there was the evidence that came out against Florence during the inquest: Mary Ann indicated that Florence had been faking sleep when she went into the bedroom to wake her. 'I think she was asleep,' she said, in court. Then she smiled and added: 'At least, her eyes were closed.' Clearly, the maid believed that Florence had been feigning. Furthermore, Florence had given six different explanations for her husband's collapse: the horse-ride; anxiety over shares; fainting fits; eating something that disagreed with him; internal inflammation; and, finally, 'a mystery'. These might have been dismissed merely as confusion on Florence's part, a legitimate attempt to find a rational explanation for her husband's illness. But it became another matter entirely when she persisted with her theories long after being told by the doctors that he was poisoned.

And so the evidence against Florence seems overwhelming. She had the motives. She had the access and the opportunity. Furthermore, my research has produced historical evidence that strongly links her with the poison.

But before we can say incontrovertibly that Florence Bravo committed the murder, we should remember that there is still one overwhelming obstacle to such a conclusion. Indeed, in the final analysis, Florence is *cleared* of killing her husband by a curious and unforeseen twist in the drama.

Dr Johnson told the inquest that he had drunk from Charles Bravo's water jug about four hours after Bravo's collapse. He had suffered no ill effects. 'I was feeling thirsty,' Dr Johnson said. 'There was a bottle on his table with a tumbler next to it. I drank at least a full tumbler of the water.'

This appeared to confuse things. It meant either that the jug had *not* been the agent of transmission, as the police believed. Or it meant that the jug had been replenished with clean water after Bravo had drunk from it – and before the first doctors had arrived. Since the police had established that there was no other vessel from which Bravo could have been poisoned, we must conclude that the murderer replenished the poisoned water soon after Bravo's collapse. How had they accomplished this? No one admitted to touching the water jug. Nor had anyone been seen refilling it. So the jug must have been refilled secretly, almost immediately after Bravo's collapse. And it is this which rules out Florence as the killer: *at no point was Florence left alone with the water jug*. Both Mary Ann and Mrs Cox were already in the sickroom when she entered it. And she was not left alone in the room from then on. She could not therefore have replenished the jug without being seen. For this reason, any sequence of events that casts Florence as the murderess is flawed by a single, logistical problem. The case against her short-circuits at the last, vital moment.

And so the question remains: What really happened that night at the Priory?

CHAPTER FIFTEEN

The Shadow on the Ceiling

I've come to close your door, my handsome, my darling,
I've come to close your door and never come again.
The shadow on the ceiling will not be mine, my darling,
So if you wake in terror, cry some other name . . .
'Bereft Child's First Night', Frances Bellerby

We may be fairly certain that Charles Bravo did not kill himself. No motive existed for him to do so and his behaviour was not consistent with such an idea. We may also be fairly certain that none of the domestic servants in the house killed him, or that he was killed by Dr Gully or an agent of Dr Gully. The mechanical problems in such theories mean that they can easily be dismissed. We are therefore left with just two suspects.

The first suspect is Mrs Cox. The evidence against Mrs Cox is that she told a number of clumsy lies on the night of the murder. The evidence in her favour is that she had no motive for killing Charles Bravo.

The second suspect is Florence Bravo. The evidence against Florence is that she had several strong motives for killing her husband, and unlimited access to the rare poison that was used. The evidence in her favour is that she could not have overcome the logistical problem in the murder – the emptying of the poisoned water jug.

A number of possible theories can be distilled out of this assessment of the facts. The first is that Mrs Cox killed Charles Bravo because she feared that her mistress's health would be fatally impaired if the marriage continued. The second is that Florence Bravo bribed Mrs Cox to carry out Charles's murder. Either of these theories succeeds in reconciling Florence's motives with Mrs Cox's behaviour.

But the problems that arise out of these two possibilities quickly become apparent. Mrs Cox may have intuited Florence's unhappiness with her marriage. But by what right did she interfere to the extent of poisoning Florence's husband? And would the comfortable Mrs Cox really have risked her life – and the position of her three children – by accepting a bribe for murder?

There was something else. Mrs Cox's behaviour might have been suspicious. But in a sense, that counted in her favour. A shrewd and clever woman like Jane Cox would have premeditated her crime. The lies she told on the night of the murder indicate that she had been caught off guard, and was having to deal with a situation for which she had made no preparation. That also ruled her out as the killer.

So we are in a situation in which Florence Bravo had the motive, but Jane Cox told the lies. How can these two features of the case be reconciled? And in reconciling them, can one discover the truth? The solution, I suggest, is as follows.

When Florence Campbell married Captain Alexander Ricardo her expectations of married life were high. She had been born into wealth and social position. In addition she had been taught that if she learned the female 'accomplishments', and if she kept herself sexually chaste, then she would be rewarded by the appearance of a good husband. Florence, we know, worked hard at these things. She studied horticulture, became a skilled horsewoman, travelled abroad, read novels and biographies, and learnt needlework. And it was not long before an appropriate candidate appeared.

Ostensibly, Ricardo seemed ideal. He was rich and well-connected, with glamorous antecedents. There can be no question that the marriage was arranged. The Campbells abbreviated the normal length of courtship in order to accomplish it. But in doing so they simultaneously left their daughter in a vulnerable position. A lengthier courtship, after all, would have exposed Ricardo's weaknesses.

The marriage ran into trouble almost at once. Ricardo drank. He was also violent. On top of this he suffered all the most distressing symptoms of alcoholism, including delirium tremens, which is usually enough to unnerve even the hardest drinkers. He was not exactly the respectable bon viveur that the Campbells had hoped for.

For Florence, the first strike of Ricardo's fist across her face must have been a transforming experience, leaving a lasting blackness in her psyche. At that moment she would have realized that there was a colossal contradiction between her invented image of married life and its coarse, violent reality. For some time Florence seems to have struggled on. Married women from her social background were under an obligation to tolerate any abuse that they received from their husbands, and to comply with close family efforts to conceal it. At first Florence seems to have been no different. Her mother says that Alexander's alcoholism was a problem from the beginning of their marriage, which meant that Florence endured about seven years of abuse. Yet there was no talk of separation until Alexander was almost dead on his feet. In fact Robert Campbell actually engaged the legal machinery necessary to drive his daughter back into the custody of a man whom he knew to be a violent alcoholic. There was no more telling exemplification of the brutality of ruling traditions.

Florence's first marriage is an important piece in the jigsaw of Charles Bravo's murder in a psychological sense. It shortened Florence's fuse. It was the failure of her married life to live up to her original expectations that was to be instrumental in her decision to commit murder. Whilst she could have absorbed the shock and humiliation of one disastrous marriage, she found it impossible to come to terms with a second.

Florence's worst fears about Charles Bravo were confirmed within weeks of their wedding: Bravo was spoilt, brutal, penurious, and foul-tempered. He was the sort of man to whom your mind would instinctively turn when you were told that someone had been expelled from your club for cheating at cards.

Anyone seeking to justify Bravo's actions after his wedding faces a gruelling task. He treated his wife as if she were marginally more significant than the servants. He bullied her whenever she resisted him. He 'persistently' sodomized her, and he threatened her life by refusing to allow her to limit her pregnancies. In due course Florence decided that she had to bring a permanent end to her marriage. Once Charles had thrown his final tantrum, on the journey to London, it became merely a matter of choosing the right moment.

On the afternoon of Tuesday, 18 April, Charles went out for a horse-ride. The horse bolted four miles with him in an effort to throw him off. When Bravo returned to the Priory he was so shaken that he had to be helped in and out of his armchair.

It seems likely that this episode gave Florence the germ of an idea. She decided that there was no reason why her husband's unfortunate experience with the horse shouldn't turn out to be unexpectedly fatal. Here was the ideal cover, after all, for a 'sudden illness'. Florence saw that her energetic husband was now so shaken that he had to be supported into the house by the groom. He couldn't even walk up a flight of stairs. All the staff noticed his condition. This, then, was surely the moment to strike.

From her own experiences with antimony she knew that a massive dose of tartar emetic would suppress the central nervous system and lead to heart failure. More importantly, she also knew that the symptoms produced by a huge dose of antimony strongly resembled those of a heart attack, and that, in at least two recent cases of antimonial murder, the physicians who had been summoned to see the patient had immediately diagnosed a routine coronary. When Bravo collapsed, therefore, the first thing that people would think of was the horse bolting. If he died from heart failure that night then there was the strong possibility that his death would be put down to the accident. The butler, Rowe, remarked later that Charles's collapse 'was fully accounted for in my mind by the horse-ride earlier in the day'.

It was, of course, a hopeless plan: the outlandish product of a mind deceived by its own grievances. But Florence was tired enough and frightened enough to blot out its flaws. There was just enough in Charles's condition for her to will herself into believing what she *wanted* to believe. 'He was so weak,' she said. 'I had never seen him look so ill.'

That evening Florence drank more than a bottle of sherry at dinner. This was in addition to whatever she had been drinking when she came home from London. On her way up to bed she asked Mrs Cox to bring her some wine, and later she asked Mary Ann to do the same. She was obviously trying to steady her nerves.

The poisoning itself would have been a fairly straightforward matter. She knew that it was Charles's habit to take a drink of water last thing at night. So, while he sat alone in the morning room, she asked Mrs Cox to go back down to the dining room and fetch her a glass of marsala. Alone on the first floor, she went to her bedroom, scooped up the little sachet of emetic, and slipped across the landing.

She emptied the sachet into the water jug, swirled it round a couple of times, and then threw the empty packet onto the fire that was burning in the grate. Then she returned to her own room. It was now a matter of simply waiting for him to go to bed.

At this point, we can begin to gauge the extent of Mrs Cox's role in the drama. It is no use pretending that Mrs Cox was *not* involved in Bravo's murder. She lied about discovering him. She lied about his confession. She procrastinated over sending for help. She misled the medical team. She dissimulated over his symptoms. And she destroyed material evidence. It is only the precise extent of her complicity that has to be determined.

We can start from the simple premise that Mrs Cox had no idea of what Florence had just done when she settled herself onto the stool by her bed. It was only as the next few moments unfolded that she understood what had happened. This is a straightforward deduction from the evidence: one of the most striking features of Mrs Cox's behaviour on the fatal night is its chaotic nature. Her actions are characterized by confusion and ineptitude. This is striking because Mrs Cox was the most organized and the least inept person in the house. If she had known about Florence's plans in advance, then the events at the Priory would have run much more smoothly. She would have made sure that Bravo was unable to raise the alarm. No doctors would have been summoned. Evidence would have been produced to support her claim of suicide. But none of this happened. From the moment that she was alerted by the maid, Mrs Cox acted as if she had been caught off guard, and was struggling to control a situation of which she had had no prior warning.

There can, therefore, be only one plausible explanation. When she heard her husband walk up the stairs and close the door of his bedroom, Florence panicked. She realized that she had reached the point of no return. The last link was broken. She could no longer govern events. The terror that this evoked in her would have been overwhelming. High drama can produce delirious confusion or a crystal lucidity. Florence suddenly grasped that her own explanation for Bravo's death was hopelessly inadequate. There was nothing for it but to confess to Mrs Cox what she had just done and to plead for her help. Mrs Cox – in the desperation of the moment – was emotionally blackmailed into helping a young woman who commanded both her gratitude and her sympathy. Consequently, she took charge and did the best she could. It is for this reason that Mrs Cox's efforts to conceal the crime aroused so much suspicion. Florence had dictated events. But it was Mrs Cox who was called upon to accommodate them.

For Florence, faced with a sudden haemorrhaging of nerve, there was nothing more natural than that she should ask her companion to step in. After all, it was Mrs Cox who had saved her life after the abortion. It was Mrs Cox who had nursed her through her repeated miscarriages and depressions. And it was Mrs Cox who had supported her in the clashes with her husband. If Dr Gully had once played a paternal role in Florence's life, then, in the same way, Mrs Cox had become her mother figure. There was no more obvious person for her to turn to in this moment of crisis. 'I do not know what I should do without her,' Florence had written to her father, five days before Bravo's poisoning.

For Mrs Cox there could be no question of anything but absolute loyalty. She was bound to her employer by ties of deep friendship. 'I liked her,' she said. 'I had great affection for her . . . We were on terms more intimate than is usual between a companion and mistress.'

'Would you have considered it wrong to have lied?' she was asked at one point.

'I did not think of myself,' she replied. 'I thought only of Mrs Bravo.'

Furthermore, Mrs Cox may have felt compelled to save Florence for another, sentimental reason: it was she who had introduced her to Charles. It was she who had encouraged their courtship. It was she, in the final analysis, who had been more responsible than anyone else for the Bravo marriage – and so for the subsequent distress that her mistress had suffered. So Mrs Cox felt driven to act.

Mrs Cox knew at once that Florence's explanation for Bravo's illness would fool no one. But she also knew that any attempt by the police to establish a motive for the murder would – if she herself remained silent – draw a blank. No one but Mrs Cox could provide concrete evidence of a motive on the part of Florence Bravo. The servants would remain silent. There were no professional or social contacts to leak evidence against her mistress. It was a world of concealed miseries. In that short moment before Charles Bravo closed the door on his room – and his life – Mrs Cox decided exactly where her loyalties lay.

A little before 10 p.m., Charles retired to his room.

He put on his nightshirt and brushed his teeth. Then he drank from the water jug on his bedside table. After that he went to the fireplace, took down the bottle of laudanum, and rubbed some of it onto his gums. He also 'swallowed a little for the pain in his face'. Then he climbed into bed.

Almost at once he would have begun to feel ill. The antimony brought 'violent pains in the stomach and a feeling of dizziness'. The dizziness would have convinced him that the cause was laudanum poisoning. He had inadvertently swallowed too much. He climbed out of bed, threw open the door of the bedroom and went out onto the landing. He called out twice for hot water. Then he went to the window of his room, put his fingers down his throat and tried to vomit.

In the main bedroom Florence and Mrs Cox remained where they were, frozen. If the alarm was raised, then Bravo would be revived. Doctors would be summoned. He might even recover. But if things were left to run their course, he would quickly slip into unconsciousness. He would either choke to death on his own vomit or die from the effects of the poison. So the women stayed where they were, breathlessly hoping that no one else in the house had heard his cry.

But neither woman had allowed for the presence of the maid. The maid's gentle insistence that all was not right in the reaction of the two women was to prove one of the most damaging points against them – or at least it would have done if the police had grasped its significance. When Bravo's shouts failed to elicit a response from his wife, the maid went into the bedroom to rouse her, startling both women. Florence faked sleep. But the maid saw through that.

Now it fell to Mrs Cox to take over. Her first task was to cover Florence's tracks. She sent the maid away on a series of useless errands – making coffee when they could not even open his mouth, searching for camphor and liniment in places where a meticulous companion would know they were not kept – so that she had a moment alone in the bedroom in which she could empty the remains of the water jug onto the rain-soaked roof, and then rinse and refill the jug with fresh water from the adjacent water closet.

Her next task was to make sure that Bravo did not survive long enough to contradict any story she could invent. In order to do this she had to delay obtaining help for as long as possible. And then she had to make sure that the doctors were ill-equipped to deal with the situation when they did arrive. So she sent for the further physician instead of the nearer. She did not tell the coachman the nature of the illness. So the doctor did not come prepared. When he appeared she did not tell him anything that might lead him to conclude that Bravo was suffering from poison. In fact she actively hindered that diagnosis. She removed his soiled nightshirt. She rinsed out the sick bowl. She kept silent about the vomit. And when Bravo passed a bloodied motion in front of the doctor she even suggested that the blood was red burgundy.

Mrs Cox's extraordinary actions provide us with further evidence that she was acting on Florence's behalf. To protect her employer, Mrs Cox fabricated a scenario in which she had privileged access to the reasons for Bravo's illness. But the actual events of his illness could not accommodate that story. Gradually Mrs Cox became mired down in her own lies – over the 'confession' at the window and over her statements to the physicians. Yet at this point Florence Bravo did not join the chorus of disbelief that was aimed at her companion: she actually leapt forward to defend her. Herein lies the confirmation; *Florence's endorsement of Mrs Cox's outlandish statements would never have been forthcoming if Florence had not engineered the crime.* What, after all, would be the normal reaction of an innocent woman whose husband was dying of poison in suspicious circumstances and whose senior domestic servant had been found to be fabricating evidence about his death? The normal reaction of an innocent person faced with such a situation would be to press vigorously for an investigation, to demand that explanations be given, to seek justice. Yet Florence expressed none of those reactions. Quite the reverse. She supported every statement that Mrs Cox made; she supported every lie, every contradiction, every act of deceit and misrepresentation. She would not have done that unless she was the instigator of the crime. Those who have previously identified Mrs Cox as Charles Bravo's murderer have consistently failed to account for this obvious fact.

But it was not just Mrs Cox's complicity that saved Florence. There was also Bravo's own dazed and ambivalent reaction to his condition, caused by the nature of his illness. After he had regained consciousness, in the early hours of his ordeal, he instinctively blamed laudanum for his symptoms. That was a natural deduction on his part. He could recall swallowing laudanum for his toothache. He could recall feeling ill afterwards. He therefore assumed that laudanum was responsible for his condition. In addition to this, there were no symptoms evident to Bravo that could contradict his assumption. He did not know that he had been vomiting blood. Nor did he see the bloodied stools that he had passed while unconscious. He was aware only of swallowing laudanum, calling for hot water, and then collapsing.

Bravo's belief that laudanum was poisoning him is also borne out by the butler's evidence. He said that when Bravo was regaining consciousness he muttered, 'No laudanum, no laudanum . . .'. Royes Bell recalled that Charles refused to accept laudanum as a pain-killer. 'He spat it out,' observed Bell, 'on being told what it was.' Dr Johnson also noted that 'when he was offered laudanum to ease his suffering, he resisted by raising his hand in a most decided manner.'

In due course, we know, Bravo's confusion subsided, and he was able to absorb the news that he hadn't been poisoned with laudanum. But by then a wave of depression had already begun to wash over him, and he was indifferent to the terrible implications that that statement carried.

In the last hours of his life Bravo wept and offered prayers for his salvation. He died, utterly exhausted, two nights after his original seizure. He had regained consciousness. But he never regained any real measure of lucidity.

Of course, the complexities of what had occurred, the inter-weaving of one person's motives with a second person's actions, meant that the true story of who had poisoned Charles Bravo, and why, was too much for those present at the Priory that night to grasp. Criminal conspiracies invariably produce legal conundrums. It is usually impossible for an outsider to unravel the extent of responsi-bility between the conspirators if they deny complicity.

A contemporary illustration of the scene at his deathbed shows that Charles Bravo died by candlelight. The last thing that he would have seen, the last image that would have flickered across his consciousness as he lay dying in that tiny bedroom, were the movements cast by the flame.

These were the shadows on the ceiling.

CHAPTER SIXTEEN

Conclusions: Under the Veil

It is sometimes said that there is no need to look further for a motive when the parties are married. Married people usually treat each other with external decency, good humour and cordiality. But what lies under the veil is known only to themselves, and the relationship may produce hatred, bitter in proportion to the intimacy it involves.

SIR JAMES STEPHEN,
History of the Criminal Law, volume III

It is a matter of historical fact that most convicted poisoners in western civilization have been women. Of a half-dozen well-known murder cases in England in the nineteenth century, in which women were the sole defendants, one of the victims was suffocated, one was shot, one perished from stab wounds, and the remaining three were poisoned. The disparity that exists between the sexes in terms of sheer physical power meant that women who intended to kill were forced to eschew direct assault in order to be successful. This also meant that women largely premeditated their crimes. It is hard to find a single case in which a female defendant is accused of killing a man during a sudden quarrel.

Interestingly, it is also a matter of historical fact that most women who were tried for murder were either acquitted or did not hang. The fact that most women used poison must have been a significant factor in acquittals. Poisoning, before the development of sophisticated means of forensic detection, was always difficult to prove. But there were other reasons: legal attitudes towards women were more lenient. Empirical research shows that Home Secretaries were far more willing to commute a woman's sentence than a man's. And women had other, subliminal means at their disposal to assist them in avoiding conviction: they could exploit the vague notions that still existed in Victorian society that respectable women were incapable of such acts, that they were creatures of immense moral rectitude, above temptation or criminality.

Insofar as there was a discernible pattern in the murderous behaviour of nineteenth-century women, it featured two striking aspects: the first was the use of poison; the second was the manipulation of popular myths in order to avoid detection. An unhappy woman with easy access to weedkiller had to be watched carefully.

Looking back, we can see a handful of reasons why Charles Bravo's death was never solved by his contemporaries, or, indeed, by the array of armchair detectives who wrote about the case.

One reason lay in the wholly inadequate system of policing that existed at the time. The files of the Metropolitan Police and of the Home Office, which run into hundreds of pages, give some indication of the problems that dogged the officers in charge of the case, and of the general limitations under which the Victorian police operated. The police failed to do anything about Bravo's death until eight days after it had occurred, by which time Florence and Mrs Cox had had the opportunity to formulate a strategy for checking the official inquiry. The fact that there were no eyewitnesses to Florence's fatal action that night, a common problem in poisoning cases, meant that the police were forced to fall back on circumstantial evidence, itself an unreliable line of prosecution. Even then, the police could not get the motives right.

But the women also escaped indictment because of the subliminal illusions about their sex that were present in popular culture. It would seem that neither the police nor the inquest jury could bring themselves to believe that someone of Florence Bravo's position and breeding could commit murder. By repeatedly underlining her educated demeanour, the obviously high cost of her clothes, her jewellery, her large house, and her army of servants, Florence was able to exploit the notion that a woman of her social position could not possibly have carried out such an act. The same unconscious reactions applied in a different way to Jane Cox. When Mrs Cox appeared in court dressed entirely in black, and acted out her evidence in a cool, rational and authoritative manner, she was clearly playing on all the unconscious prejudices that accompanied the jury's image of her professional status. Here was a woman who had spent her life looking after children, who had worked for rectors and curates, solicitors and barristers, a woman whose occupation embodied all the high moral principles upon which society itself was founded. Such a woman was surely incapable of lying. Of course, Mrs Cox's evasiveness under cross-examination may have tested this belief to the limit. But the thinking behind it was rooted in an emotional logic that was irrational anyway.

At the same time, Florence was also able to use her talent for duplicity in order to avoid detection. Indeed, the extent of popular belief in her innocence is a remarkable tribute to her skill at mendacity. All the doctors and lawyers believed her. We know that the doctors and lawyers involved in the case spoke strongly during the inquest in favour of her 'convincing reactions'. 'Her behaviour was generally consistent with innocence,' said the Crown counsel, Sir Harry Poland. 'I saw no trace of feigning on her part,' said Dr Johnson. 'Her reactions were entirely natural,' recalled Royes Bell. But it is significant that those who believed in Florence's innocence were, with the exception of Joseph Bravo, all men.

Florence's ability to lie convincingly was not merely an inherent part of her make-up as a person. She was neither more nor less deceitful than her contemporaries. Rather, her talent for duplicity came from her social development. Invention was an integral part of life for women of her time, who were encouraged from an early age to conceal their opinions, their emotions and – especially – their desires. They were also expected to camouflage their bodies, and to keep secret any mysterious functions their bodies might perform. Furthermore, women were forced to resort to deception by the overt male oppression around them. Like any social group under constant threat, and with limited means of resistance, they used it as a means of survival. Florence Bravo had been brought up by an overbearing father, and had been married to two brutal men. She had naturally become very skilful at exploiting masculine gullibility. It is significant that the only person she seemed unable to fool was another woman – the maid, Mary Ann Keeber.

The case of Florence Bravo remains almost unique in the canon of celebrated nineteenth-century women. In an age where women enjoyed no legal status and no enshrined rights within marriage, her radical attitudes to marital roles were startlingly different from those of her contemporaries. Beneath the public attacks on her for her sexual misdemeanours lay an even more conservative seam of criticism, condemning the challenges that she had made to the masculine status quo.

This was an age in which women were deprived of some of the most basic human rights. They did not have the vote. They had no legal status in the workplace, no trade unions to protect them (because they were largely unskilled), and no social organizations to join. At the same time women lacked any professional opportunities. Marriage was deemed to be a woman's only goal. Those who remained unmarried and supported themselves had to be content with domestic work. No university admitted women. They were excluded from the professions. They could get no training to develop artistic, scientific or commercial talents.

Women were also denied real freedom in choosing a partner, too, and had no power within marriage. Their lack of professional opportunities meant that they were forced to marry for cold, synthetic reasons – money, respectability, the continuation of the family line – and their own romantic designs were always a lesser consideration in the struggle to attain these goals. Once married, they were expected to endure almost any degree of domestic unhappiness – even if it included habitual violence. They could not obtain divorces. And they had great difficulty in securing the custody of their children if they separated from their husbands. Women had no property or money of their own. Even their earnings belonged to the man of the house.

Against this background, then, Florence Bravo was a singular social phenomenon. She was a public figure whose behaviour strongly defied established convention, and who was always prepared to bend the rules to get what she wanted. When her first husband became violent, Florence did not meekly accept the abuse. She left him. When her father tried to intervene, she cut herself off from her family. When she fell for James Gully she did not suppress her longing because both parties were still married. She took him to her bed. And the self-assertion continued after she met Bravo. Bravo's insistence that he be master in his own house was a convention so commonly accepted that it barely needed articulating. Yet Bravo was anything but the master. Florence resisted his domestic management, criticized him for his penury, challenged his right to dismiss employees and refused to give up her luxuries. She even had the audacity to remind him that *she* was the one who 'found the money for things'.

There was no more obvious example of Florence's radicalism than her reaction to Bravo's mistress. A man's sexual infidelity in the nineenth century was a much less serious issue than his wife's – indeed, it was almost a trivial matter. A man might have any number of mistresses and still be a respected member of the community. And that was how men liked it. But it was different for women. A woman fell at the merest whisper of a sexual taint. She became a social pariah. This hypocrisy reached its apotheosis with the French Napoleonic Code, which disqualified men from being tried for murder if they killed their wives after discovering that they had committed adultery. The same law did not apply, of course, to those wives who committed murder upon discovering that they had adulterous husbands.

But Florence would not tolerate these double standards. She reacted against Bravo's taunting of her over her lost affair and reminded him that he too had enjoyed an illicit lover. 'We had made

an agreement,' she said. 'But he was constantly bringing up Dr
Gully's name, and always upbraiding me for my association with
him. I said I thought it a very cruel thing that he was always bringing
up Dr Gully's name. I said: "I am not always talking to you about
that woman."'

It would be wrong and implausible, I think, to suggest that
Florence's attitude to her marital situation characterized her as some
sort of radical feminist. But it is certainly true that her attempt to take
control of her life, to ignore traditional conventions, foreshadowed a
pattern of social change which, though still in an embryonic stage,
was steadily gaining ground.

The claim that Florence's story exposed the problems with which
many Victorian women were familiar, even if the solution she
employed was not, is supported by the degree of interest amongst
women in her 'trial' at the Coroner's court. Women were notorious-
ly avid devotees of criminal proceedings, so much so that both
journalists and social commentators had begun to attack what they
perceived to be an 'unfeminine' prurience prevailing amongst
women newspaper readers as early as 1850. At the time of Madeleine
Smith's trial in Scotland, a journalist wrote that women readers who
followed the proceedings in the newspapers 'dishonoured their sex
by eagerly drinking in that filthy correspondence'. And in 1864, the
year that Florence married Alexander, a novelist noted:

> ... that women of family and position, women who have been
> brought up in refined society, women who pride themselves upon
> the delicacy of their sensibilities, who would faint at the sight of a
> cut finger and go into hysterics if the drowning of a litter of kittens
> were mentioned in their hearing – such women can sit for hours
> listening to the details of a cold-blooded murder.

As we know, it is true that the Victorians were fascinated by sensational murder cases. But the interest amongst women in domestic
murders could not be dismissed merely in terms of bloodthirsty
prurience. It was more complex than that. Their curiosity stemmed

from the evidence that the proceedings exposed about domestic conditions which they recognized within their own lives. The simple fact remained that the courtroom revelations of marital circumstances which had led certain women to kill their husbands often strongly mirrored the experiences of women sitting in the gallery as spectators. They were fascinated by the spectacle of the accused women taking extreme measures to resolve domestic conflicts similar to their own.

'I told him that he had no right to treat me in such a way,' said Florence, in her Treasury statement, referring to her husband. No woman in England heard that remark when it was read to the Coroner's court, since, by then, women had been banned from attending the hearing. But they read it in their newspapers and in their pennysheets, and they heard it from their friends. And though they may not have sanctioned the dark and terrible remedy to which Florence Bravo had, in her sickness and misery, succumbed, some part of them understood it.

Her words, it might be said, were their own.

A Dozen Broken Lives

The scandal broke us all. The Campbells were ruined by what had happened. Within a few years the whole family went bankrupt and Robert's health collapsed. So many lives were changed.

ALISON HARRIS, great-great-granddaughter of Robert Campbell, January 2001

The story of Florence's last days was a testament to the power of social disapproval. Her death, less than two years after the inquest, amounted to a virtual suicide. But its route had been a slow and painful one.

Immediately after the inquest, Florence returned to the Priory. She watched as Mrs Cox packed her bags and left the house. Gradually, her family melted away, too, her father returning to his sick-bed at Buscot, her brother William setting out for Australia. William implored his sister to go with him, to start a new life, free from the shackles of the past. But Florence had been running for most of her life – from Alexander, from Gully, and then from Bravo. She decided to remain in England and submit to the will of events. Perhaps she knew already that she was finished.

In due course, the servants also left the Priory; Mary Ann the last to go. A short time later she received notice from the landlord of the house that he would be taking legal steps to evict her. There was a strange irony to that. Two years earlier, when she had married Bravo, she had written to the landlord, asking him to revoke the terms of their agreement. She had wanted a fresh start then, and was conscious of Gully's presence down the road. She had even tried to persuade Gully to give up the lease on his own house and return to Malvern. But Gully had remained where he was. And the landlord had refused to accept notice on Florence's tenure.

She later told her family that she would have left the Priory anyway; she knew that she was irretrievably disgraced in that small community, and that there could be no hope of re-establishing herself. It was not simply that the jury had, in the eyes of her neighbours, condemned her as a murderess – the verdict, after all, was akin to the Scottish verdict of Not Proven; it was much more that she could not hope to recover from the damage done to her reputation by the sexual details that had emerged during the cross-examinations. The revelations had electrified the entire country. Florence had been publicly humiliated in an age whose watchwords were discretion, concealment, reticence. She was a social pariah, beyond the pale.

Florence left Buscot at the end of September and returned to London to arrange the sale of her furnishings. She contacted Bonham and Son, the Prince Street auctioneers, and asked them to sell off the entire contents of the Priory: the furniture, pianos, busts, prints, china, cutlery – everything; even the cellar of wines that Charles had carefully built up. She wanted nothing to remind her of her old life. She changed her surname to Turner. At the same time, she began to search the south coast for a suitable house to rent. Finally, in the spring of 1877, she was ready. She drove away from the Priory on 3 April, leaving Balham and London for ever. She would not be heard of again until her death.

Eventually she settled in Southsea, Hampshire. She had chosen Southsea for several reasons. She had a fondness for the south coast that reflected the preferences of her social group: Worthing, Brighton, Eastbourne, Southsea – these had been the chief catchment areas for the Victorian upper classes at leisure. She had also holidayed there with Gully. He had praised the benefits of the sea air on her constitution. And her name was less notorious amongst the local society than, say, at Brighton or Worthing, where she had been a regular visitor during her affair and her second marriage.

In order to find out what I could about her life after the inquest, I drove to the city library at Portsmouth, in Guildhall Square, where local newspapers and civic archives were kept. These showed that Florence Turner had arrived here in April 1877, and had bought a property called Lumps Villa, on the sea-front. Florence had changed the name of the house to Coombe Lodge, but I could find no Coombe Lodge on town maps or postal records, and no Lumps Lane, which was the address listed in the archives. Later, I discovered that Lumps Lane had been changed in 1901 to Eastern Parade. This meant that my hotel, the Solent, which was on the sea-front, was less than a hundred yards from Florence's old house. I found it that evening, in warm summer rain, encircled by modern flats, looking mournfully across the mouth of the harbour.

Florence had hired a small staff on her arrival at the villa – a housekeeper, Mrs Everett; two maids, Anne Spanner and Jane Parton, and a coachman. But it was clear that her reclusion at Southsea had been total. There had been no contact with her neighbours, who rarely saw her, and no attempt to establish a footing in local society. According to the maids she rarely left the house.

At the end of the summer, when she had been in Southsea just four months, a doctor was summoned by the housekeeper to attend Florence, who was said to be suffering from fever and nausea. The doctor was surprised to find that his patient was actually suffering from the effects of too much brandy. He told her to watch her consumption, to eat properly, and to think about taking a holiday. He also told her to get out more. But the doctor's casual response in fact ignored a serious problem. Florence had developed a taste for sherry during her second marriage. Perhaps it had helped her to cope with the abuse. And she was encouraged in the habit by Mrs Cox, who had an amazing capacity for consuming liquor. Inspector Clarke had once noted that 'both Mrs Bravo and Mrs Cox are greatly given to drink', but Mrs Cox seemed to have the kind of constitution that could tolerate large quantities of alcohol. Florence, on the other hand, did not. Two weeks after he had first been called out, Dr Smith was back at the villa, attending his patient again. Now she was complaining of abdominal pains. She was coughing up a heavy black fluid from her stomach. The alcohol was eating away at the membranes, exactly as it had done to her first husband, almost ten years earlier. Although she was only thirty-two, Florence was abusing her body in a manner that was potentially fatal.

The doctor was more concerned now. He told the servants not to let Mrs Turner have any more brandy or wine. He also contacted her parents and expressed his misgivings about her emotional state. The young woman was drinking herself to death, he said.

The occupants of Buscot remained disconcertingly calm about Florence's plight. But it was indicative of their own serious troubles. Mrs Campbell was already trying to deal with the ill-health of her husband, who was suffering from pneumonia. The Park was in financial trouble, seriously over-capitalized, and Robert Campbell had collapsed from the strain of overwork. 'Perhaps Anne Campbell felt that she had done enough for her daughter,' said Alison Harris, 'helping her to avoid a criminal charge. Perhaps she felt her efforts were now needed closer to home.' At any rate, no one from Buscot visited. But Mrs Campbell did finally contact Florence's uncle, her own brother, James Orr, who lived in Scotland, and asked him to go to Southsea to assess her daughter's condition.

James Orr arrived in the summer of 1878. He was shocked by Florence's appearance: she had lost weight; her face was grey and drawn; she did not seem to be properly nourished. The servants had been unable to resist her orders for brandy and gin, he was told. Orr checked into a local hotel, the Royal Beach, and decided to extend his stay. He discussed a holiday with his niece, and was pleased to find that she seemed open to the idea. He then spoke to Dr Smith. He also told the servants that on no account was Florence to be allowed any spirits at all.

The following day Orr arrived at the villa to take afternoon tea with his niece, a routine that had become established since his arrival. He found Florence too drunk to speak to him. He also found that the housekeeper, Mrs Everett, had left. Florence later insisted that she had been unsuitable, and had gone by mutual agreement. But Orr was suspicious. He discreetly cross-examined the maid, Anne Spanner, and found that Mrs Everett had in fact been sacked by Florence for disobedience. 'She told me that Florence had asked her to fetch a bottle of brandy from the town,' he recalled, later, 'and she had said that she was under orders not to do so.' Florence had retaliated: 'You take your orders from me. You will fetch me brandy or you can have a week's notice.' In the event, Mrs Everett had stood her ground, and Florence had then dismissed her.

Two days later, the performance was repeated with the maid. But the maid's circumstances did not permit her to demonstrate the housekeeper's resolve.

> Mrs Turner said to me: 'Has Everett gone?' I said: 'Yes, Ma'am, she has.' Then she said: 'Do you know whether she has gone out of Portsmouth?' I said I did not know, she had not said where she would be going. Then Mrs Turner said: 'I want you to get me a bottle of brandy.' I said: 'Oh, Ma'am, you know Mr Orr said you were not to have it.' But she said: 'I will have it, and you are to send for it.' I tried to discourage her by telling her that the gardener . . . who usually carried out these errands, had gone home for the day. But she said I must fetch it myself.

James Orr said that he had arranged to take his niece to Scotland on Friday, 13 September. But when he arrived at Coombe Lodge, Florence was lying on the sofa, incapacitated. 'She was in a poor way,' he said. 'She had a reasonable constitution, but it was affected by drink. Sometimes she would be vomiting for several hours. She took drink until it caused her to vomit and then she was obliged to leave off it.' Over the weekend, Orr said, Florence continued to drink; her condition worsened, and she began to vomit dark fluid from her stomach. 'After that,' said Orr, 'the two servants could hardly keep life in her.' Orr arranged for the housemaid to nurse Florence through Monday night, but when he called on Tuesday morning, the day of her death, she had deteriorated badly.

'On Tuesday morning I called to see her at six o'clock,' he said, 'before my sea-bath. I went there at that early hour because I felt anxious about her. In spite of her condition, she pleaded with me for alcohol. She was lying on the sofa and she said: "Oh, do give me a little, or I shall die." I keep a little flask of brandy in my pocket, and as I saw she was faint I gave her a little.

'I did not notice any real change in her condition,' he went on. 'She was very pale and breathing heavily, as was always the case after heavy vomiting. I saw what came off her stomach: it was heavy black fluid. This carried on throughout the day. Her breathing was very bad. She said she was very tired and remarked, "I'm going, I'm going."'

It was not until after lunch on that Tuesday that Orr realized his niece was dying. 'I didn't think that the case would be fatal until the Tuesday afternoon,' he said. 'That was when I began to have my doubts about it. I thought at first she would recover, the same as she had done before. The collapse which led to her death was sudden — around 2 p.m.'

'When you saw her sudden collapse,' asked the Coroner, 'did you then send for Dr Smith?'

'No, I didn't,' replied Orr. 'I asked her if I should send for him, but she said no. I also asked her if I should send for her mother. Again she shook her head and said no. About an hour before her death she began vomiting black fluid again. Then she cried out, "Oh, I can't breathe! Oh, save me, save me!" I then went and got a spoonful of brandy and gave it to her. She died shortly before four o'clock in the presence of myself and two servants.'

Dr Smith, giving evidence after James Orr, said that he had assisted during the post-mortem, which had revealed that Florence's heart, liver, and kidneys were in a 'degenerated condition', and that severe internal bleeding had taken place through the walls of the stomach. 'Death was due to haemorrhage produced by violent vomiting, and accelerated by a weakened heart,' he said. 'Excessive use of stimulants produced violent sickness, which strained the stomach and ruptured the vessels.' Subsequently, the jury recorded a verdict of Death by Misadventure.

Two months later, Florence's will was read. Money was left to

Jane Cox's three sons and to James Gully's granddaughter, Florence, to whom Florence Bravo had been godmother. Her personal effects were scattered amongst her family, and the bulk of her estate was left to her brother William and, in trust, to his descendants.

The game of consequences was over.

One hundred and twenty years after the scandal, I drove down to Buscot Park on a blisteringly hot afternoon in July. The temperature was in the eighties, and the landscaped park was in bloom. Inside, the house was cool and dim, the marble floors and cotton drapes offering some relief from the heat. The drawing room was a masterpiece of Regency style, which Campbell had designed on his arrival, with gilt furniture and tall, Kentian pillars. In the master bedroom there was a copy of the bible belonging to Florence's sister, Effie, inscribed with her name.

Buscot had been sold in 1887 by Robert Campbell's trustees and had been bought by a financier, Alexander Henderson, later the first Lord Faringdon. Henderson was an art collector, and the house now contains one of the largest art collections in the country. Henderson's son was a passionate socialist, and Buscot became a meeting place for leaders of the Labour Party – a fitting purpose for a house rescued and rebuilt by an early Reformist. Today it is owned and managed by the National Trust.

Members of Florence's family described to me in some detail how the scandal had ruined the lives of their ancestors. 'They were greatly affected by what had happened,' said Alison Gordon. 'They never really recovered from what they saw as a sordid and shaming affair.' Robert Campbell's poor health was worsened by the inquest and the legal struggle to protect his daughter. 'It really broke him,' said Alison Harris, Robert's great-great-granddaughter. 'He lost half a million in the space of a few years and went bankrupt. My own great-grandfather – Florence's brother – had to sell the family estates here in New Zealand to help clear the debts.'

'Robert left less than two thousand pounds to each of his children,' Diana McManaway told me. 'Everyone was shattered by what had happened. Rarely has such an ancient and powerful family collapsed so quickly.'

From Buscot, I drove west to Malvern, through Oxfordshire and up into Worcestershire, towards the Welsh hills. Malvern today is a shrine to its greater past. On arrival there I took tea in Gully's old clinic, now the Tudor Hotel, in the same rooms where the doctor had treated the distraught Florence Ricardo, 125 years earlier. The picturesque bridge that separated the clinic's male and female quarters, the famous Bridge of Sighs, still stands, and the gardens of the clinic are as beautiful and as exotic as those that Gully originally designed.

Gully's only son, William, entered the House of Commons as a Liberal MP, and was voted Speaker of the House three times. Dasent's *Lives of the Speakers* records that Tory MPs shouted, 'Bravo, Gully!' when he entered the chamber to take his seat.

All of the senior legal and medical figures involved in the case flourished. Dr Johnson was appointed President of the Royal Medical Society in 1884 and Physician Extraordinary to the Queen in 1889. He was knighted in 1892 and died four years later.

Sir William Gull remained the most senior physician in the country until his retirement through illness in 1887. He died of a stroke in 1890. In his will he left £344,000, an estate unprecedented in the history of medicine. Almost a century after his death, the author Stephen Knight published a book in which he claimed that Sir William Gull had been Jack the Ripper. The book, which became an international best-seller, contended that Gull had eliminated a number of women who were attempting to blackmail the Crown over a secret liaison between a prostitute and the Duke of Clarence.

Sir Henry James, Florence's counsel at the inquest, became a leading member of two successive Liberal administrations. In 1880, when Gladstone was returned, he was reappointed Attorney General, an office that he had first held two years before the Bravo inquest. He died in 1909.

Joseph and Mary Bravo never did return to Jamaica. Mary Bravo died within fifteen months of her son's death. She was forty-eight. *The Times* records her death on 16 July 1877 from 'enlargement of the liver and haematemesis', and notes that she been 'bed-ridden since the death of her only son last year'. Joseph Bravo outlived his wife by four years. His will, in which he left the bulk of his vast fortune to Charles's two sisters, was proved in London, on 21 July 1881. Meanwhile, Bravo's cousin and best friend, Royes Bell, outlived him by less than a decade, dying, aged forty, in 1886. When I located Bell's will at Somerset House I found that it had been drawn up by Charles Bravo, in his own hand, and that it had been witnessed by both Charles and Florence.

Bravo's two closest friends – Frederick MacCalmont, who had walked back along Piccadilly with him on the day of his poisoning, and Edward Hope, with whom Bravo had shared chambers at 1, Essex Court – had met strikingly different fates.

I managed to trace Hope's granddaughter, now in her eighties, living on the south coast. Her son, Viscount Mersey, assisted my research into Bravo's professional career by arranging for family records to be checked. Hope's granddaughter told me that her grandfather had had a long and distinguished career in public life. He had left the practice that he had shared with Bravo in 1879, she said.

It seemed extraordinary to me that I was speaking to someone whose grandfather had known the central characters of the story; who had himself been an important witness at the inquest.

Bravo's other close friend, Frederick MacCalmont, met a bizarre death just a few years after his friend. He had established himself as a political authority in 1879 with the publication of his *Parliamentary Poll Book*, which remains in print and is regularly updated. Two years after its publication, however, MacCalmont killed himself with an accidental overdose of chloroform, which he had been in the habit of using as a sleeping agent.

*

Mrs Cox did not die in Jamaica, but eventually chose to return to England with her youngest son, Henry, leaving John and Charles to manage the family estates. A newspaper that ran an article on the case in 1949 received a letter shortly after publication from a Mr Carmley, then aged seventy-eight, living in Brighton. Mr Carmley said that he had known Mrs Cox when he had worked in the town as a bank clerk, just before the First World War. 'She often came to see me,' he said, 'and brought fruit and things for my father, who was ill.' This account rings true: Mrs Cox had had two sons at school in Brighton and knew the town well.

In the spring of 2001 I travelled to Jamaica to find the plantation estates of the Cox family. I flew into Kingston and drove through the parishes of St Catherine and St Mary to the north of the island, where Mrs Cox and her sons had made their home. At St Ann's Bay, I visited the local library to search records and maps relating to the history of the area. Then I drove deep into the interior, many kilometres south of the coast, to find Content, the family home. I finally traced it to an area around Lime Hall, a mountainous land-scape of rocky uplands and dense, fertile valleys. The estate was still functioning as a pimento plantation – exactly as it was when Mrs Cox had settled here. But it had long ago been broken up into small freehold plots, each cultivated by the descendents of slaves.

I stopped at a roadside pub, no more than a tin shed, where a handful of labourers were drinking and playing cards in the late afternoon sun. A heated argument, leavened by raucous laughter, was briefly suspended as I aproached. This was not tourist Jamaica, with its hustlers and hermetically-sealed hotels: this was the rural outback, where white faces were as rare as snowfalls. But the drinkers were pleased to welcome a stranger; they were knowl-edgeable and happy to chat. The Cox family, they said, had been important figures in the area for many years. Their property stretched for more than a thousand acres, and they had enjoyed great wealth. Mrs Cox's son, John Leslie, had married a native Jamaican and his Creole ancestors still lived in the area. The family had cultivated pimento, a staple berry for export. Henry Cox, a great-great-great grandson of Jane Cox, now farmed in the area south of Content, producing crop for the perfume industry. The house itself, the fine colonial property that had stood in the hills overlooking the lush tropics of the bay, had been demolished soon after John Leslie's death. Only a ruined plot remained. Mrs Cox's second home, Endeavour, a wooden mansion with verandahs and wide Regency windows, had burned to the ground in the last twenty years. But a third house, Carlton, had survived, down in the district of Moneague, where the family had grown tea and citrus fruits.

Back in St Ann's Bay, driving through the town centre, there were more echoes of the past. The trip down from the hills carried me into Gully Road – the doctor's father had also farmed here – and a little way along, now bustling with school-children, lay Bravo Street, the location for St Ann's famous courthouse, named after Charles's stepfather.

Secrecy, in different ways, surrounds the burial places of all four protagonists of the Bravo story. Jane Cox lies in an unmarked grave in Hither Green Cemetery. 'We have her plot registration,' an official from Lewisham Borough Council told me, 'but the grave is not marked.' Dr Gully took deliberate steps to conceal the whereabouts of his remains. While dying from cancer in the spring of 1883 he arranged for his body to be buried in secret. 'He clearly didn't want anyone to know the location of his grave,' said Janet Grierson, a Malvern historian. 'And to this day we still don't know where his body lies.'

Florence, too, was buried in private. After her death, her parents and her brother William conspired to keep hidden both her funeral arrangements and the sight of her grave. Her body, it is popularly said, was conveyed by train not to Faringdon, the most convenient station for Buscot churchyard, but to Challow, seven miles away. The coffin arrived there in the early hours of the morning, and was driven straight to the churchyard. The servants, it is claimed, were sworn to secrecy as to the nature of their work.

The legend seems believable. An extensive search of St Mary's churchyard at Buscot, conducted by the author on a windswept February morning, confirmed that Florence's grave remains un-marked.

Fifty miles away, meanwhile, at West Norwood Cemetery, mystery also surrounds the site of Charles Bravo's remains, though here it is an unforeseen consequence of time and nature. The large surround that stood over his grave has collapsed. The engraving on the stone – Sacred to the Memory of Charles Delauney Turner Bravo – is barely decipherable. Bracken and brambles entwine around the stone, claiming it back into the earth. In five years, the site of Charles Bravo's grave will have vanished under a mass of foliage, and his last resting place, like those of the others, will be unknown.

NOTES

General sources
The bulk of my quotations are taken from transcripts of the Coroner's inquest, held in Balham between July and August 1876. Other sources are indicated in the text or these Notes. Copies of correspondence from this period, including the letter that Florence wrote to Mrs Cox on 23 August 1873, are also sourced from the inquest coverage. The proceedings of the inquest were extensively reported in the contemporary press, with only minor verbatim discrepancies. The best and most reliable source remains *The Times*, then distinguished as the nation's paper of record.

For the pattern of social history I have consulted academic research undertaken in England and the United States in the last thirty years, including *Modernisation of Women in the Nineteenth Century* by Patricia Branca and Peter Stern, published by Forum; *Silent Sisterhood: Middle-Class Women in the Victorian Home* by Patricia Branca, published by Carnegie-Mellon Press; *Victorian Murderesses* by Professor Mary Hartman, published by Robson Books; and *An Economic and Social History of Britain* by Trevor May, published by Longman.

CHAPTER ONE: THE BRIDGE OF SIGHS, PP. 9–31

Florence Campbell
This is the first book on Florence Campbell to have been sourced directly from members of her own family, to whom I remain grateful for their help and cooperation. Most of the descendants connected with this case are from the family of William Campbell, Robert's second son and Florence's elder brother. William and Florence had a close relationship and his descendants in New Zealand are custodians of the family archives. (When Robert Campbell excommunicated his daughter during her affair with Gully, William was the only one of five brothers and three sisters who defied his father and remained in contact with Florence. He also supported her during the inquest and in the last years of her life.) When she died in September 1878, Florence left her fortune to William and to his daughter, Margaret. Margaret went to live in New Zealand at the end of the nineteenth century, dying there in 1951, and I have traced and inter-

viewed her grandchildren. Margaret's eldest granddaughter, Alison Harris, helped me greatly, as did her sister, Diana McManaway. Margaret remembered Florence well, having been brought up at Buscot, and she has passed information on to her grandchildren about Florence's life. Much of the new evidence in this book comes from these sources.

Additionally, other descendants of Robert Campbell returned to England after his bankruptcy, and are scattered throughout the United Kingdom. As well as speaking with Janet McKellar, a descendant of Florence's younger brother, Stuart, I also contacted Angus and Alison Gordon, descended through Robert's eldest son, who gave me further information on Florence's life and marriages.

Florence and Alexander
For background information on the story of Florence's first marriage I have drawn on my own interviews with members of the Campbell and Ricardo families. I have also relied on accounts given by witnesses during the Coroner's inquest.

James Gully
My sources for the life of James Gully are numerous. I interviewed several local historians at Malvern, including the author, Cora Weaver, and the crime writer Richard Whittington Egan. I also consulted David Edwards, from the *Malvern Gazette*; Dr John Harcup, a GP who has written about Gully, and many others. There have been several books devoted to the life and works of James Gully, as well as those describing the nineteenth-century history of the Water Cure. The public library at Malvern has privately published papers on the subject and a great deal on James Gully's medical career. The library also has an extensive local history collection, outlining the development of hydrotherapy in the town.

James Manby Gully studied medicine in Paris and at Edinburgh University. He had awards from L'Ecole de St Barbe in Paris and from L'Ecole de Médecine. Gully's life had been changed overnight in 1842 when he had read a paper by the Austrian surgeon, Vincenz Priessnitz, who was an advocate of hydrotherapy. He had at once given up his surgery in London, and, with the help of another hydrotherapist, James Wilson, established a Water Cure clinic at Malvern.

In his landmark study, *The Water Cure in Chronic Disease*, Gully had outlined his thesis: disease was largely the result of internal organs being acutely or chronically 'congested' with excess blood. The Water Cure — water consumption, baths and wet sheets — stimulated the nervous system to alter the circulation and relieve the congested tissues. But it did not end there. The treatment also represented a reaction against the notorious excesses of Victorian domestic life. It stressed exercise, strict diets, relaxation, and sleep. In an age when over-indulgence and lack of hygiene were universal, the strict discipline of the Water Cure inevitably produced dramatic improvements in almost every patient. It was no coincidence, Gully noted, that in England, where nervous disorders appeared more prevalent than on the continent, 'productive economy and good government' had 'dramatically increased the indolence and leisure of the higher classes'.

Within ten years of the founding of their first clinic, Gully and Wilson had become national figures. Patients came from Europe and the United States. A second clinic was opened in 1852, and a third in 1854. But it is significant that it was Gully, and not Wilson, who attracted the social glory. Although Wilson had actually founded their first clinic, Gully was the more engaging figure: an articulate public speaker and writer, much in demand on the dinner circuits and in the literary milieu of London society. Interestingly, the *Post Office Directory* of 1852 gives a clear indication of the social distinction that he had attained: the Worcestershire issue classifies him under the heading 'Gentry', whilst other doctors in the county are classified as 'Physicians', and placed under 'Trades'.

Gully's first famous patient was Alfred, Lord Tennyson, who arrived in 1847, aged thirty-eight, suffering from anxiety and depression. Charles Darwin arrived the following year 'unable to do anything one day out of three'. He and Gully became close friends and Darwin made frequent social calls on the doctor during the remainder of his life. Charles Dickens came next, in 1851, followed by Thomas Carlyle, Florence Nightingale, Thomas Attwood and Samuel Wilberforce. Information on celebrated patients in Gully's practice can be found in John Harcup's book, *The Malvern Water Cure*; in Eleni Odescalchi's *Charles Dickens in Malvern*; *Tennyson and Malvern* by Elizabeth Jenkins; and *Florence Nightingale* by Cecil Woodham Smith. The public library at Malvern has further records of interest, dealing with visits by Lord Aberdeen, Disraeli, Gladstone, Bulwer Lytton, and others.

Although Gully believed that the Water Cure, or the hydropathic treatment, could help significantly to reduce some of his patients' problems, he also believed that part of the solution lay in altering the very status of women in contemporary society. He was an advocate of a whole range of female causes: temperance, for instance, because of the brutalizing effect of alcohol on husbands; votes for women, to widen participation and provide a sense of purpose. Gully placed such importance on the need for women to be free from masculine-oriented pressures that, at Malvern, males and females were strictly segregated into separate clinics. The clinics were divided by the quaintly named Bridge of Sighs.

Florence and Gully

Florence's affair with James Gully has been massively covered in publications and electronic media devoted to the case. Again, I have consulted the Campbell family for information on this area. It was the Coroner's inquest that revealed the full extent of Florence's involvement with Gully, and the history of the relationship. Florence admitted committing perjury during the first day of her cross-examination, claiming to have been James Gully's lover just once, during the visit to Kissingen in November 1871. The next day she confessed to 'other occasions' of intimacy, 'more than once'. Although she went on to insist that her abortion had been a miscarriage, her claim was contradicted by Mrs Cox, who told the jury how Dr Gully had arrived at the Priory to remove what he described as 'a kind of tumour'. According to Professor Mary Hartman (*Victorian Murderesses*, Robson Books), Gully himself was rumoured to have prescribed abortifacient drugs to his female patients.

Florence and the Priory
Florence's lifestyle after leaving the Hydro was nomadic. She spent some time at a villa in Graham Road, Malvern, before checking into the Crystal Palace Hotel, London. After this she stayed with her solicitor, Henry Brooks, as a paying guest at his Surrey home, Brooklands, before moving to a furnished house in Leigham Court Road, Streatham, called Stokefield. She finally took possession of the Priory on 21 March 1872, securing a twenty-one-year lease. The details of the furnishings of the Priory can be found in the catalogues of Bonham and Sons, September 1877, now in the British Library.

Mrs Cox
Jane Cannon Cox was born in Chester in 1827, the eldest daughter of a merchant from the East Indies. Her mother ran a girls' school in Bebington. She claimed to have been born with the surname Edouard, giving her French connections, but her birth certificate at Somerset House shows this to be untrue (it was probably a device that she employed to enhance her status as a governess, since familiarity with French literature and language were much sought after as qualifications). After the death of her husband in Jamaica in 1867 she returned to England and founded a ladies' seminary in Woodbridge, Suffolk. When the seminary failed she worked as a governess before joining Florence, beginning her employment on 25 May 1872.

CHAPTER TWO: GAMES OF CONSEQUENCE, PP. 32–41

Details of the Married Woman's Property Act can be found in *An Economic and Social History of Britain* by Trevor May, published by Longman, or, indeed, in any standard textbook on the period.

The epigraph on page 32 comes from a letter written by Florence to Charles, dated 21 October 1875. The letter was read out during the Coroner's inquest.

The issues surrounding the status of married women in Victorian England have been the subject of lengthy discussion. See Notes, Chapter 1.

The episode involving George Griffiths was explored at some length during the inquest, when Griffiths himself gave evidence. The manager of the Bedford Hotel, Charles Stringer, was also called as a witness and asked to repeat verbatim his exchange with the coachman.

Florence's apology to her father was contained in a letter she wrote to him on 25 October 1875.

Charles Bravo

For details of Charles Bravo's background, I have consulted the genealogical study, 'Collections for a life and background of James Manby Gully' by Phyllis Mann, a private paper that remains unpublished but which can be found in Malvern public library. The paper outlines the author's lifelong attempt to trace the ancestry of all the principal characters in the Bravo story, some of them dating back to the eighteenth century.

Further studies of Bravo's character can be found in 'The Balham Mystery', a Victorian pamphlet privately published in August 1876, now in the British Library.

CHAPTER THREE: THE MISTRESS OF THE HOUSE, PP. 42–53

Florence and Charles's marriage

There are two principal sources of evidence for the deterioration of Florence's marriage: her own four-page statement given to the Treasury Solicitor on 1 June 1876; and Mrs Cox's statement to the same officer, also given on the same day. Both statements form part of the Home Office files on the case, which can be found at the Public Record Office in Kew. Additional evidence about the Bravos' marriage comes from the inquest testimony of Anne Campbell, Florence's mother, the only member of her family to enter the witness box. Her evidence can be found on page 12 of *The Times*, 25 July 1876. Bravo's attitude to his wife's domestic expenditure was outlined by her in the Treasury statement and supported by Mrs Cox. The butler also endorsed her claims about Bravo's penury, saying that he had heard them rowing over 'cheques which Mr Bravo was not disposed to write out'. Further evidence comes from the exchange of letters between Mary and Joseph Bravo and their son, detailing Florence's 'excessive' expenditure and the need for 'retrenchment'.

Florence's statement is surprisingly explicit. But she has problems with chronology and continuity which neither her own solicitor, George Brooks, nor the Treasury Solicitor appear to have ironed out. She is naturally reticent when referring to her sexual relationship with Bravo.

Florence and Charles's sex life

This aspect of the Bravos' marriage has remained largely unexplored, for obvious reasons. At the time of Bravo's death, no feature of the couple's sex life was publicly disclosed in spite of the enormous interest in their marital relations, and this has remained the case throughout the history of subsequent investigations. But two separate sources which I have identified – the first, Florence's inquest testimony, the second, the police report of Chief Inspector Clarke of 22 May – provide us with incontrovertible evidence that Bravo was habitually buggering his wife throughout their five months of marriage.

The first piece of evidence came from a cross-examination that took place during the Coroner's inquest. Florence was asked by the Crown QC, Sir John Gorst, whether she had made 'serious allegations' and 'grave charges' of a 'highly personal nature' against her late husband during her consultations with Dr Dill. Florence agreed that she had. But she was unwilling to elaborate on them in court. 'It is not the sort of thing I would want to discuss with any man,' she said, 'except a doctor.' The jury assumed that this cross-examination referred to syphilis. But they later heard from the police pathologist that there had been no trace of venereal disease on Bravo's body. Subsequently, the Coroner demanded that the jury put the question from their minds.

The assertion that the cross-examination actually referred to anal intercourse, however, is supported by evidence from the police files, which confirms that the 'grave charge' that Florence had made against her husband arose because 'he engaged in a persistent line of conduct'. Anal penetration would certainly constitute 'a grave charge'. It had been a capital offence in England for 900 years. It would also cause the kind of health problems that Florence would not wish to discuss 'with any man except a doctor'. Additionally, the phrase 'line of conduct' was widely used by prosecution counsels to describe anal sex during cases brought against those committing 'the abominable crime of buggery', as the Statute amusingly described the offence.

Sexual studies were obviously not performed in Victorian England, so it is impossible to provide empirical evidence to support the claim that anal sex was widely practised within marriage. But a great deal of anecdotal evidence has been unearthed by academics which suggests that it had become common. 'Rubber goods', as they were usually known, were not widely available until the end of the First World War, when social campaigner Marie Stopes began petitioning for their sale in chemists. For the Victorian woman with a sexually active husband, the question of birth control presented a problem; consensual anal sex was a relatively safe remedy. Studies that have addressed these issues, and estimate the extent of the practice, include Ronald Pearsall's *The Worm in the Bud: The World of Victorian Sexuality*, published by Macmillan; and *Sex and the British* by Paul Ferris, published by Michael Joseph.

CHAPTER FOUR: 'AN EXTREMELY DANGEROUS WOMAN',
PP. 54–64

Mrs Cox's dismissal
The sources for Bravo's plan to dismiss Mrs Cox are numerous. Joseph Bravo told the Coroner's inquest: 'He discussed with me the expense which Mrs Cox was on his household. I agreed that it was not wise to subject the establishment to that charge.' On 12 February 1876, Charles himself, away at Sessions on the Home Circuit, wrote to Florence: 'By putting down the cobs *and* Mrs Cox we could save £400 a year.' Florence told the inquest: 'He was always pressing me to turn away Mrs Cox, to save money.' Rowe, the butler, said: 'There was an understanding in the household that Mrs Cox had [received] notice. She had no particular duties, only fetching anything that Mrs Bravo wanted.' On 7 August 1876, Mrs Cox's friend, Ellen Harford, told the inquest that Mrs Cox had discussed her situation, including Bravo's plans to dismiss her, during a long conversation in the previous spring. Curiously, Florence's reaction to Bravo's plan to dispense with Mrs Cox's services is not recorded.

The prescription for laurel water
Details of this curious incident were first brought to the attention of the police by Mrs Campbell, with whom Mrs Cox had discussed her meetings with Dr Gully. Both Gully and Mrs Cox were extensively questioned on the meetings and the laurel water at the inquest. 'It was harmless,' Mrs Cox said, at one point. 'I believe it is sometimes given to children.'

CHAPTER SIX: 'A MOST PERPLEXING ILLNESS . . .', PP. 70–84

Bravo's death
The account of Bravo's death is amongst the most well sourced in the whole story. All the principal figures involved – family members, servants, doctors – gave their recollections of those three days to the Coroner. The exchanges of dialogue that I have reported are sourced directly from these testimonies. Additionally, Dr George Johnson, who took charge of the patient, wrote an extensive account of events, including clinical details of symptoms and treatment, for the *Lancet* magazine in August 1876. Copies are available at the Wellcome Medical Library of the History of Medicine and the British Library. Further details of Bravo's illness were drawn from the files of the Royal College of Surgeons and the Royal College of Physicians, including the clinical notes of Dr Johnson. A lengthy article on the symptoms which Bravo exhibited, together with the progress of his illness, can be found in the *British Medical Journal*, 1973, volume 122, a copy of which can be accessed from the Library of the Royal Society of Medicine. Additional clinical information on

antimony can be found in *Antimony in Medical History* by John McCallum, published by Pentland Press.

CHAPTER SEVEN: THE INVESTIGATION, PP.85–95

Scotland Yard's inquiry

The progress of Scotland Yard's inquiry is outlined in the official police reports at the Public Record Office. Clinical details of Charles Bravo's autopsy, which was performed on 22 April 1876 at St Thomas's Hospital, were provided to the Coroner on Monday 24 July 1876 by Joseph Frank Payne, FRCP. Professor Theophilus Redwood's evidence, covering the chemisty of antimony tartrate, was given on Friday, 14 July 1876.

The inquest

All quotations from witnesses at the inquest are given verbatim from *The Times* between 11 July and 11 August, 1876. A further discussion of the case followed in the newspaper's readers' column, and included additional remarks on the case given by – amongst others – Royes Bell and Dr Johnson. Historians of the case will be surprised by my heavy editing of the inquest proceedings. This was a publishing decision; all the principal findings of, and exchanges during, the inquest have been included in the other areas of the book; but to have lingered over an inconclusive inquiry would, I felt, have infuriated the reader and fatally slowed the narrative progress of the story. Detailed accounts of the inquiry can be found in the three full-length studies of the case listed in the Bibliography or in coverage provided by *The Times* and the *Daily News*.

It should be noted that a preliminary inquest had been held in April 1876, and had returned an open verdict, but that the Coroner, who did not call Florence as a witness and neatly filleted the proceedings of controversy, was forced to hold a second inquiry after petitions were made to the Home Secretary by Bravo's family. Mrs Cox also precipitated a second inquiry by claiming that Bravo had committed suicide because of his jealousy of Dr Gully.

CHAPTER NINE: 'THE CURIOUS DEMEANOUR OF THE DYING MAN', PP.109–18

The book that propounded the suicide theory was *Recollections of Forty Years* by Dr L. Forbes Winslow, a London psychiatrist.

Dr Andrew Haynes is Director of the Institute of International Finance and a senior lecturer in the Department of Law, the University of Wolverhampton. Dr Benjamin Jacoby is a senior industrial biochemist based in Buckinghamshire. At the time of writing, Dr John Vale is Director of the West Midlands Poisons Unit, City Hospital Trust, Birmingham.

Please note that copies of *Martindales* are, as a general rule, only available to clinicians.

Dr Johnson's account of the drug therapy administered to Charles Bravo is given in the *Lancet* magazine, 30 August 1876.

The cross-examination of Sir William Gull took place during the Coroner's inquest on 14 July 1876. Other quotations from physicians are also taken from their evidence to the Coroner's inquest.

Sir William Gull was exposed as a high-ranking Freemason by Stephen Knight in his 1985 book, *The Brotherhood*. Knight does not make reference to Robert Campbell or Joseph Bravo as being Freemasons, but Campbell's status – particularly his appointment as High Sheriff of Berkshire and as Berkshire Justice of the Peace – make it almost inconceivable that he would not have enjoyed Masonic connections. 'I did not know Mrs Bravo,' said Sir William. 'But I knew Mr Campbell very well as a patient and an acquaintance.'

CHAPTER TEN: NOT MURDER, MANSLAUGHTER, PP.119–23

Professor Mary Hartman is now Director of the Women's Studies Institute, Rutgers University, New Jersey, USA. Our interview took place on 25 May 2000. Professor Hartman's theory is expounded in some detail in her groundbreaking book, *Victorian Murderesses*, originally designed as an academic study, but written with such verve and style that it quickly became a best-seller (see Chapter Four: The New Women – Florence Bravo and Henriette Francey).

Elizabeth Jenkins now lives in retirement in Hampstead, London. She has written widely on the case, her first publication appearing more than fifty years ago.

Adelaide Bartlett was tried for murder in London in the spring of 1886. *The Times* newspaper gives a full account of the proceedings, as does the author Yseult Bridges in her 1962 book, *Poison and Adelaide Bartlett*. The quotation from the trial comes from Dr James Leach and was given in evidence on 9 February 1886, during the trial of Mrs Bartlett.

CHAPTER TWELVE: ABOVE SUSPICION, PP.127–34

The epigraph comes from an article on the case by Elizabeth Jenkins, published in October 1968 in *The Sunday Times*, to which Agatha Christie contributed.

For information on James Gully's philanthropy and civic career in Malvern I have relied on Pamela Hurle's *Portrait of Malvern*, and Phyllis Mann's unpublished private work, 'Collections for a life and background of James Manby Gully', which is in the collection of the Malvern public library. (I also consulted

Ms Mann's series of articles, 'Dr Gully and the Bravo Case: a reassessment of factors in the mystery', published in four weekly parts by the *Malvern Gazette* in May 1977.) My sources from Malvern include Cora Weaver, a local writer; Richard Whittington Egan, a crime writer living in the town; Janet Grierson, a local historian; and two reporters from the *Malvern Gazette*, David Edwards and Simon Evans.

CHAPTER THIRTEEN: 'A GOOD LITTLE WOMAN', PP.135–47

During my visit to Jamaica I traced archives in the National Library, Kingston, and the Jamaica National Archives in Spanish Town, where colonial records and property directories of the nineteenth century are stored. The list of files that I consulted are noted in the Reference Sources.

During my stay I also visited St Ann's Bay, where the Cox family properties are located. Carlton and Endeavour lie seven miles to the west of Ocho Rios, as does the family home, Content, where Jane and her sons lived their impressive, colonial life. I also visited the town's courthouse, where records show that Jane Cox appeared in August 1879 as executrix of the will of her aunt, Margaret. A short walk from the building is Bravo Street, named after Charles's stepfather.

I have arrived at estimates of Mrs Cox's fortune by extrapolating the estate records, which I researched while in Jamaica, at the National Archives, giving the value of Jamaican land at the time. In the 1840s, worn-out coffee plantations were being sold at £6 per acre. In March 1846, an estate in St Ann's Bay was sold for £3 per acre. In 1855, an estate in Port Royal was sold for £6 per acre. Of course, thirty or so years later, the value of the land would normally have risen considerably. An 1876 valuation at £10 per acre would have put the value of the Cox property at well over £12,000. However, the 1870s was a hard time for colonists on the island. Many of their staples had crashed. Landlords were finding the value of their land had diminished. It would be unwise, therefore, to estimate the value of the Cox property beyond £5 per acre. This is a reasonable figure, especially given that St Ann's Bay had resisted the worst of the crashes (in the mid-century, it was one of only two counties on the island to have over 1,800 new peasant freeholds). Furthermore, when Jane Cox inherited the property, in 1879, there was a huge surge in the number of small freeholds in the north, substantially increasing the value of her land. I have not included the value of the houses in this calculation. (More details of acreage valuations can be found in Professor Tim Holt's study, *The Problems of Freedom: Race, Labor and Politics*.)

CHAPTER SIXTEEN: CONCLUSIONS: UNDER THE VEIL, PP.171—7

Madeleine Smith was charged with murdering her lover, Emile L'Angelier, in the spring of 1856. It was alleged that she had poisoned him with arsenic, which she stirred into his coffee, after he had threatened to expose their love affair to her father, a respectable Edinburgh businessman. She was acquitted under the Scottish verdict of Not Proven. The sexual element in the story created a national sensation, especially when Madeleine's letters to her lover, describing her pleasure on the numerous occasions when they had had intercourse, were read out in court. The quote condemning female spectators is taken from the *Daily Express*, 15 July 1856. The quote on page 176 comes from *Victorian Studies in Scarlet* by Ricard Altick, published by Norton.

Women were banned from the Bravo inquest during the evidence of Florence Bravo and Dr Gully on the insistence of Sir John Gorst, who felt that the tone of the proceedings might have a corrupting influence on the 'delicate sex'.

AFTERMATH: A DOZEN BROKEN LIVES, PP.178—89

Details of Florence's last days in Southsea can be found in the *Portsmouth Times & Naval Gazette*, September 1878. 'No one knows to this hour,' says the paper, when reporting her death, 'whether she died with a secret, [and] whether it was a secret which rendered alcohol a necessity.' Copies of the newspaper are on microfilm at the Portsmouth Public Library, Guildhall Square. Florence's death was also reported in the *Evening Standard* during the same month.

Details of the lives of the lawyers and physicians involved in the case can be found in the relevant editions of *Who's Who*. Details of the death of Frederick MacCalmont were obtained from the obituary page of *The Times*, 12 February 1881.

REFERENCE SOURCES

BOOKS

Biron Henry, Chartres, *Without Prejudice*, Faber & Faber Ltd, 1936.

Bridges, Yseult, *How Charles Bravo Died*, Jarrolds Ltd, 1956; reprinted with new postscript, 1971.

Clarke, K., and Taylor, B., *Murder at the Priory*, Grafton Books, 1988.

Forbes Winslow, L., *Recollections of Forty Years*, John Ouseley Ltd, 1910.

Gully, Dr James Manby, *The Water Cure in Chronic Diseases*, Malvern, Henry Lamb; London, Simpkin, Marshall & Co., 1846 and 1863.

Gully, Dr James Manby, *The Water Cure in Acute Diseases*, Simpkin, Marshall & Co., 1863.

Hall, Sir John, *The Bravo Mystery*, The Bodley Head Ltd, 1923.

Harcup, Dr John Winsor, *The Malvern Water Cure, or Victims for Weeks in Wet Sheets*, Winsor Fox Photos, 1992.

Hartman, Professor Mary S., *Victorian Murderesses*, Robson Books Ltd, 1976.

Holt, Professor Thomas C., *The Problem of Freedom: Race, Labor and Politics in Jamaica and Britain 1838–1842*, The John Hopkins University Press, 1992.

Hurle, Pamela, *Portrait of Malvern*, Phillimore, 1985.

Jenkins, Elizabeth, *The Balham Mystery*, Sampson Low, 1949.

Jenkins, Elizabeth, *Dr Gully*, London, Michael Joseph, 1972; published in New York as *Dr Gully's Story*, Coward, McGann & Geoghegan, 1972.

Lowndes (formerly Belloc), Marie Adelaide, *What Really Happened?*, Hutchinson, 1926.

Mowbray-Berington, Merle, *The Saturday Review, 1858–1868: Representative Educated Opinion in Victorian England*, Columbia University Press, 1941.

Porter, Roy (ed.), *The Medical History of Waters and Spas*, The Wellcome Institute for the History of Medicine, 1990.

Rickard, Jessie Louis, *Not Sufficient Evidence*, Constable & Co., 1926.

Sayers, Dorothy, *et al*, *Great Unsolved Crimes*, Hutchinson, 1938.

Shearing, Joseph, *For Her to See*, Hutchinson & Co., 1947.

Smith, Brian, *A History of Malvern*, 1st edn, Leicester University Press, 1944, 2nd edn, Alan Sutton, 1978.

Sturge and Harvey, *The West Indies in 1837*, Frank Cass & Co., 1968 (first edn, 1838).

Veal, F. J. P., *A Verdict in Doubt: The Bravo Case*, Merrymeade Publishing Co. Ltd, 1950.

Williams, John. *Suddenly at the Priory*, William Heinemann Ltd, 1957; reprinted with minor revisions, 1975 and 1985.

Wilson, J., and Gully, J. M., *The Dangers of the Water Cure*, Simpkin, Marshall & Co., 1843.

REFERENCE BOOKS

Alumni Oronienses, the Matriculation Register of the Members of the University of Oxford, 1715–1886, vol. I, compiled by Joseph Foster, published by James Parker & Co., London, 1891.

Dictionary of New Zealand Biography, G. H. Scholefield, Department of Internal Affairs, Wellington, 1940.

Jamaican Almanack for 1821, Montego Bay, 1821.

Monumental Inscriptions of Jamaica, compiled by Phillip Wright, published by the Society of Genealogists, London, 1966.

NEWSPAPERS AND PERIODICALS

Daily Chronicle
Daily News
Daily Telegraph
Globe
Graphic
Hampshire Post
Illustrated Police News
Illustrated London News
Lancet
New Monthly Magazine
Pictorial World
Portsmouth Times & Naval Gazette
South London Press
Strand Magazine
The Sunday Times
The Times
Vanity Fair
World

PAMPHLETS

The Balham Mystery: A Complete Record of the Bravo Poisoning Case of 1876,
    published by the *Daily Telegraph*, August 1876.
The Gay Young Widow of Balham, Anonymous, London, August 1876.
The Bravo Case, published by *The Penny Illustrated Paper and Illustrated Times*
    special issue, 5 August 1876.

UNITED KINGDOM: GOVERNMENT PAPERS AND RECORDS

Metropolitan Police File (reg. MEPO 3/123).
Colonial Office Records (CO 137/284).
Colonial Office Records (CO 137/289).
English Census Returns, Public Record Office, London.
Index of Wills and Probates 1875–1960, Somerset House, The Strand,
    London.
St Catherine's Register of Births, Deaths and Marriages 1880–1950, General
    Register Office, St Catherine's House, London.

JAMAICA: GOVERNMENT PAPER AND RECORDS

National Library of Jamaica
Sligo Estate Papers (MS 275 D).

Jamaica National Archives
Letters of Testamentary: 1B/11/18/51 folio 304.
                            1B/11/18/55 folio 136.
Inventories: 1B/11/3/159 folio 99.
                            1B/11/3/162 folio 210.
Parish Register of St Ann: 1B/11/8/2/6 folio 196. 1849–71: nos.175 and 176,
                            and folio 232.
Return of Properties (Directory) 1882.

RADIO AND TELEVISION

The Balham Affair: a one-hour television play, first transmitted on ITV in
    1990.
An Infamous Address: a one-hour BBC documentary, first transmitted in
    October 1987 on BBC Radio 4, written and presented by Roger Wilkes.
The Poisoning of Charles Bravo: a three-part BBC television series, first trans-
    mitted in June 1975, written by Ken Taylor, directed by John Glenister,
    produced by Mark Shrivas.

INDEX

CB = Charles Bravo
FB = Florence Bravo
JC = Jane Cox
JG = Dr James Gully